Bringing Out the Best in People

How to Apply the Astonishing Power of Positive Reinforcement

Third Edition of the Classic Best Seller

AUBREY C. DANIELS

New York   Chicago   San Francisco   Athens   London   Madrid
Mexico City   Milan   New Delhi   Singapore   Sydney   Toronto

1 2 3 4 5 6 7 8 9 0   DOC   21 20 19 18 17 16

ISBN   978-1-259-64490-0
MHID   1-259-64490-1

e-ISBN   978-1-259-64489-8
e-MHID   1-259-64489-4

McGraw-Hill Education books are available at special quantity discounts to use as premiums and sales promotions or for use in corporate training programs. To contact a representative, please e-mail us at bulksales@mheducation.com.

This book is dedicated to my mother,
Carrie Belle Daniels (1913–2016),
who always brought out the best in me.

Contents

PART 4
Turning Good Intentions into High Performance

Preface

Much has changed since 1994 when this book was first written—the iPod, iPad, Skype, GPS, mobile broadband, YouTube, Bluetooth, iPhone, Facebook, Twitter, Pinterest, Instagram, search engines, smartphones, Amazon, satellite TV, and Wikipedia, to name a few. Access to information is now at everyone's fingertips. An endless amount and variety of videos, books, and articles are virtually free to anyone who owns a computer, tablet, or smartphone. Ways of communicating with people around the globe are just a few keystrokes away. In many ways the world has been revolutionized in the last 22 years.

Someone found in the jungle after being given up for dead for 20 years would find it difficult to get in the door of the average business and would be completely lost when shown his former workspace. He would not know how to turn on a computer, much less how to use it. However, when he went to Human Resources (HR), he would be right at home because HR policies are pretty much the same. Although he would be pleased with the current salary or hourly wage, the structure of the organization, policies about how to behave, and the consequences of failure to conform will have changed little.

In the first chapter of the second edition of this book, I stated that many of the current theories of management and leadership were wrong. In the intervening 16+ years, not much has happened to change my opinion. They are still wrong. And all the books, articles, and management seminars of the last two decades have done little to affect the form and practice of management.

Something else that has not changed is the laws of behavior. Behavior changes today just like it did 20 years ago. Make that more than 2,000 years ago. As far as we can tell, behavior won't change for another 2,000 years from now. We learned from our environment 2,000 years ago, and we still do. The problem is that only a very few of those who designed business environments knew the laws of behavior then and now.

This is a long way of saying that even though much has changed since 1994, much of what I wrote in the first edition is still in the third edition. In this edition, I have tried to update examples and have added three new chapters. One chapter is about technology and how it is changing behavior—sometimes for the better—and how sometimes it is creating new problems. Another chapter is about engagement because it is still a major issue in the supercompetitive business climate we find ourselves in as we enter the twenty-first century, even though businesses have been working on this for over 100 years.

Also, the examples have been updated because some of them in the first edition are unknown to many who are currently entering the workforce. Some references also have been added. The basic concepts of the science are still the same. Hopefully, some of the edits I have made will make these concepts easier to understand and apply.

In my 45 years of teaching executives, managers, supervisors, and employees the science of behavior—behavior analysis—I have often heard it referred to as a "soft" science. The implication is that it is not really a science at all. Physics, biology, and chemistry are often called "hard" sciences. In my opinion, all real science is hard science. Experimenters either follow the scientific method so that their findings can be replicated or they don't. I believe that a well-designed experiment never has a bad outcome. Even negative results add to the body of knowledge because that relationship between variables need not take time away from other important experimentation.

What is required for a finding to be scientific is not well understood, even by many academics. Many in fields of study like to think that the content they teach is not learned from random experience but from carefully constructed scientific studies. However, much of the content fails the acid tests of science—prediction and control. Sir Peter Medawar, writing on the limits of science in 1984, said, "I expect that its embarrassing infirmity of prediction has been the most important single factor that denies the coveted designation of 'science' to, for example, economics." There are more theories of behavior in psychology than there are psychologists because every psychologist has more than one.

In my blog (www.aubreydanielsblog.com) and presentations I encourage participants to look at a study to see the variables under study, how they were tested and evaluated, and the conclusions the authors draw from the data before they take something presented as scientifically demonstrated. It is not uncommon that a study is well designed, but the data do not support the interpretation.

In this book I will try to present what the research has discovered over the last 80 years or so—and do so in a way and with words that are easily understood so that it can be put into practical use. I will also try to clearly separate what science knows from what is my opinion.

Let me end with a quote from Robert Owen,[1] written in 1813:

> If, then, due care as to the state of your inanimate machines can produce such beneficial results, what may not be expected if you devote equal attention to your vital machines, which are far more wonderfully constructed?
>
> When you shall acquire a right knowledge of these, of their curious mechanism, of their self-adjusting powers; when the proper mainspring shall be applied to their varied movements you will become conscious of their real value, and you will readily be induced to turn your thoughts more frequently from your inanimate to your living machines; you will discover that the latter may be easily trained and directed to procure a large increase of pecuniary gain, while you may also derive from them high and substantial gratification.

What I intend to present in this book is a "right knowledge" of human behavior as we know it today so that businesses can realize the benefits described by Robert Owen over 200 years ago.

Note
1. Robert Owen, *A New View of Society* (1813).

PART 1

The Perils of Traditional Management

1

Fads, Fantasies, and Fixes

What if you lived in the 1980s, saved your money, moved into your dream house in an isolated wooded area with a great view, bought a new car, and everything seemed to be going your way, and then you woke up one morning and noticed that even though you went to bed early, you were still tired and had low energy. You began to feel sleepy and could fall asleep anywhere. When you told a friend about it, she asked if you had been tested for sleep apnea. You scheduled an appointment with a doctor, were tested, and the results came back negative. The doctor suggested that you might try to sleep on your side and raise the head of the bed slightly for a better rest. You tried what the doctor recommended, but after an initial improvement for several weeks, you realized that you were no better. After several months of continued tiredness and low energy, a return to the doctor resulted in a test for low testosterone. When the results came back, it was marginally low but within the normal range, but your doctor, on the side of caution, recommended using a low dosage of testosterone in the form of a patch. For several months you felt better, but after a while, you began to notice some side effects and realized that the initial symptoms were unchanged. At your annual physical, when you reported your continued problems, your doctor suggested that you should take a multivitamin with iron. The results were the same as the others: short-term benefit that soon gave way to the same tired, low-energy feelings. After many trips to the doctor with the same effect, you found yourself trying supplements you saw advertised on TV or the

Internet. After hundreds of dollars and many years of trying, you gave up and decided that this was just something you had to live with. Suddenly, it seems, it is the year 2020. You meet a new employee at work, and she asks where you live. You tell her your address, and she says it certainly is a beautiful area and she considered a house in that area until after considerable research she discovered that it was the site of a factory that made chemicals during World War II. Because it had been so many years, the records were sketchy and long forgotten. To make a long story shorter, tests revealed that toxic fumes were still present and were the cause of the problems you had been experiencing all those years. Nothing was wrong with you—you were responding naturally to the environment in which you found yourself.

What has this example got to do with business? Everything! In this example, you and your doctor both assume that the problem is *you*, and for at least the last 50 years that I have been around businesses and other organizations, the assumption that executives have, by and large, is that it's *the employee who is the problem*. Think of it this way: most companies hire the smartest, most talented and skilled people available, who are vetted every way from Sunday, and then are later discharged because they cannot or won't do the job.

We have all known employees who came to work all excited about being employed but after several months perform the job in a routine manner. I have heard it said many times, "I thought he was going to be a trailblazer, and now he is just like all the others. What's happened to him?"

Something everyone agrees with is that we learn from our environment. Regardless of our DNA or social and financial circumstances, the things that happen to us change our behavior. Unfortunately, we seem to forget this important fact when we design a workplace where an employee will spend the bulk of her waking hours during her work life. Somewhere this fact gets lost, and apart from the things companies do to make the workplace physically comfortable and safe, the environment itself gets little notice, and its effect on behavior gets lots of attention, but practically none of it is scientifically validated.

By *work environment*, I refer not only to the physical workplace but also primarily to the rules, regulations, rules of conduct, and the behaviors of supervisors, managers, and executives. Also important are processes, work systems, and the hierarchy of management. All these factors combine to have a tremendous impact on the performance of employees.

Searching Google with "engagement in business" yields 411 million hits. This is a "hot" topic today, and I predict that it will remain hot for years to come. After all, it has been a major initiative for at least 50 years. It disguises itself by various names but is engagement, nonetheless. Quality circles were the rage in the 1970s. They were replaced by Deming in the 1980s, employee involvement in the 1990s, and self-managed work teams, supervisor-less workplaces, and engagement beyond 2010. What is worse is that some of these initiatives that failed decades ago are now being recycled in the hope that they will work in the new century with millennials.

The point of this example is that if we learn from the environment, it should be the first place we look for answers to employee motivation. Often it is the last place, if it is considered at all. Every employee provides a "fit for use" test of the environment that supposedly has been designed to "bring out the best in people." This does not mean that the employee is always right or that bad behavior should be tolerated. Quite the contrary. Even though problem behavior may have been created in large part by the workplace, nothing is gained by excusing it. The guiding principle for action is, "Is the action that is taken by management likely to bring out the best in the person or more likely to create additional problems?" Such action may involve a negative response from management if that is what will be best for the person and the organization. With the science of behavior as an advisor, this book will give you specific guidance on how to create an organization that is specifically designed to bring out the best in people.

What if American management, after all these years of trying, has been dead wrong about how to manage effectively? What if the latest celebrated management theory is just another quick fix, destined to reap only short-term gains and produce long-term frustration? What if the only people benefiting from this cycle of hypothetical theories are the management gurus promising "the answer" to companies so desperate for a management approach that works that they are willing to try anything?

In 1971, Professor Joe Bailey of the University of Texas said that "the half-life of all panaceas in the educational and business worlds is seven years, plus or minus two" (*Training Magazine*, April 1993). By the 1990s, it shrank to 18 months. In the last half of the 2010 decade, it is probably about one year. And with the new computer technology delivering "new and better" every six months or so, the temptation to jump from one solution to the next—or many all at once—is even greater.

As the temporary impact of each fad wears off, no longer producing the kind of changes expected and promised, many executives drop the old and charge off in search of the new—and currently "hot"—management theory only to be disappointed in a year or so. As years pass, initiatives such as quality circles, total quality management (TQM), management by wandering about (MBWA), competencies, matrix management, Six Sigma, and emotional intelligence have had enormous popularity and after a few years have all but disappeared from the business scene. Dr. Robert Birnbaum, a professor at the University of Maryland, identified 378 fads in the field of education from 1960 to 2000! The cycle of temporary answers continues because most approaches to management are never rooted in anything more substantial than limited observations, in limited settings, over limited time periods. The lesson American management steadfastly refuses to learn is that managing by emotions, perceptions, or common sense is not really managing at all. Leaders also refuse to accept the fact that people—the very engine of the business machine—cannot be ignored or treated as expendable parts. Human performance is not a factor in a complicated equation for business success: it is *the answer* to the equation.

We all selectively perceive and retain experiences and information. We then evaluate and interpret them from a base of previous experiences and perceptions. With all these individual variables, it's obvious that those who manage only from personal experience and the thoughts and feelings that accompany that experience are subject to unpredictable results. Today's business environment demands a much more precise approach—one that produces consistent results, one that is based on science, not opinion. My concern is that business leaders will continue to treat management as a mysterious, somewhat personal art form simply because it is easier to continue to do what they learned in the past than to change it for a more effective way. There is a constant flow of leadership books presenting every conceivable analogy of the leadership challenge. One used the jazz band analogy because good jazz, like good business, requires strong leaders and strong players. This analogy holds true to a point, but good business is not an orchestral production or a Broadway show, well scripted and choreographed. Rather, it is an ongoing process requiring constant vigilance and diligence to meet the demands of an ever-changing and unpredictable marketplace.

From "My Own Style" to a Precise Procedure

The most popular management approach by far is reminiscent of a song by Frank Sinatra, "My Way." This is basically "management by the seat of your pants" or, to put it in an acronym, which seems to be required in management consulting these days, MOMS (My Own Management Style). This kind of management drives executives and human resources (HR) crazy and always creates problems for the organization.

What company can possibly succeed over the long term if hundreds of its managers have their own individual management styles? How do you know that each manager's style is going to support the company's values and mission? What chance does such an approach have to bring out the best in the workforce? Imagine a company with hundreds of different management styles. The only outcome of that situation is an environment full of rules and regulations whereby executives try to manage the problems created.

Imagine a doctor saying, "I've developed my own operational style. I'm going to operate on your brain a little differently than other surgeons would. No need to worry. I'm very comfortable with my style of operating, and I've had a couple of good successes."

Or suppose that a pilot announces over a plane's public address system, "I'm going to land this plane a little differently than FAA procedures require. I've got my own method. I feel that today the runway assigned by the control tower is not the best, so I'm going to use another. It will work out better, I assure you."

Performing surgery or landing a plane requires precision and the use of established procedures. With many businesses struggling to survive, and with large numbers of them failing, why do we tolerate so many subjective approaches to managing people? Innovation in management is not wrong, but innovation without data, management by "hunch," and "let's give it a run and see what happens" techniques are too costly to tolerate any longer.

Bringing out the best in people and achieving measurably superior results require a clear and precise understanding of human behavior. Yet most people understand the laws of human behavior at about the same level as they do the laws of gravity. They know that gravity keeps them on the Earth, and they know not to walk off the top of a tall building. But they don't know enough to send astronauts to the moon and bring them back. Most managers know enough about human behavior to know that positive methods of management are preferred to negative ones. However, they usually know very little about how the selection, delivery, and timing of positive and negative consequences in the workplace influence the way people behave.

Many managers have an immediately negative reaction when they are told that they need to study and understand human behavior. They don't believe that such study is necessary to managing a business effectively. They might as well say that they don't believe in the laws of gravity. Believe in gravity or not, when they jump, they will still come back to Earth.

If you work with other human beings, you are subject to the laws of behavior. And if you don't understand them, more than likely you're impeding, possibly depressing, the performance of your employees, your peers, and even yourself. To obtain measurably superior results in the workplace, managers must understand why people behave as they do with the same depth that rocket scientists understand gravity.

MOMS Versus Precision Management

Very few managers use systematic, scientifically based management methods to bring out the best in people at work. Most try a variety of management approaches until they find one they like. But even when that approach seems to work, they don't know exactly why it did or why it works sometimes and sometimes doesn't.

Conversely, the approach described in this book is not something that I made up. It's based on over 100 years of research in human behavior. The body of knowledge is called *behavior analysis*. Application of these scientific findings to the workplace is called *performance management* and *precision management*. Once managers understand the scientific principles, they can create a workplace environment that brings out the best in people today, tomorrow, next month, and next year.

The senior managers I've known are not particularly impressed with one-time performance improvement in a job, an office, or a factory. They know that things occasionally get better. They get interested when things improve and continue to improve.

Blue Cross and Blue Shield of Alabama has been using this form of management since 1980 and even as of this writing enrolls new supervisors and managers in training to know how to apply these scientific principles to their work in the medical insurance business. M&T Bank began using performance management in 2002, and its executive vice president now teaches the subject in a business class at the University of Buffalo.

Performance management is not a one-time management solution to a single problem at work. It provides a precise way of analyzing work and implementing a management system that not only will address the problems associated with inadequate performance but also will lead to practical ways to maximize performance in every aspect of the company's business. Because performance management is a precise, data-oriented approach, the solutions can be replicated in the same or similar settings and even can be extended to new settings with similar results.

Several years ago I visited a middle manager in a large manufacturing company. Ralph O. had been applying performance management in his department for about a year and had invited me to see the accomplishments of his team. The country was in a recession, and the company was in the midst of its second downsizing in two years. Despite the doom and gloom prevalent in other departments occupying the same building, Ralph's team was enjoying dramatic successes, reducing labor and maintenance costs while demonstrating measurable quality improvement in their product.

Even more impressive was the fact that Ralph, reading the downsizing handwriting on the wall, had gathered his department together and offered department members the challenge of improving their cost structure in a more constructive way than the usual method of mandated headcount cuts by corporate. Ralph's department found a way to reduce labor costs more than was requested, yet no one was laid off. All this improvement was accomplished through the use of performance management at a time when most people, including most of Ralph's peers and managers, thought any improvement was impossible.

During my flight home, I wrote a note to that company's manufacturing vice president. I suggested that if the downsizing got to him and he needed a lift, he should go see Ralph and let him show how he was helping the company.

Most important, I wanted that vice president to understand that what Ralph and his management team had done could be repeated in other areas. I wanted him to know that what was done did not depend on Ralph's charisma or other personal attributes. Ralph had used a straightforward process that could be taught to all managers and supervisors.

Business Is Behavior

Performance management teaches managers how to influence behavior. A company hires people because what needs to be done requires people to do it. Even in the current high-tech workplace, the behavior of people is the only way anything is accomplished in business. Even though managers don't understand behavior management methods, behaviors are changing. The only thing preventing behavior change is death. If managers and supervisors are not applying behavioral laws consciously and correctly, they are almost certainly decreasing some behaviors that they want and increasing others that they don't want.

Because every organizational accomplishment depends on behavior, whenever an organization strives to improve quality and safety, increase productivity, or boost creativity, it requires employees to change their behavior. People must then either do the same things they are currently doing more or less often or do different things. However, in order for managers to change employee behavior, they must first change their own. In order to have sustainable behavior change, everyone must change. *Consequently, the one thing executives, managers, and supervisors should know the most about is human behavior.*

Every management system ever devised was intended to bring out the best in people but failed because it violated basic laws of human behavior. If it doesn't know the conditions under which people do their best, the organization will survive only through sheer luck.

Behavior Is a Function of Its Consequences

When most people see someone do something that is out of the ordinary, they ask, "Why does that person do that?" Most of us have been trained to look for the answer in what happened *before* the behavior occurred. In other words, we think the behavior was caused—motivated—by some internal force, drive, need, or desire or by some external order, request, or signal. Because some behavior appears to occur without an apparent external motivator, we are puzzled.

A behavior analyst, however, would respond, "A person does that because of what happens to that person when he or she does it." That is, the cause of the behavior lies not in the conditions prior to the behavior but in what happens immediately *after* the behavior.

For most people, this is a totally new way of looking at behavior, but it can be very helpful because it means that you don't have to read minds or try "to figure people out." You have everything you need to understand people when you *witness the behavior and observe the consequences of the behavior.*

Psychologists study the mind; behavior analysts study behavior and how to optimize desirable behaviors. Although psychologists would say that *behavior is the window to the mind,* I prefer to leave people's minds alone. What goes on in other people's minds is, frankly, none of my business. In any event, the business of business is behavior.

A Most Practical Approach

Because performance management focuses on understanding behavior, we are able to tell what works and what doesn't simply by examining the impact an intervention has on the behavior of people. Did the behavior increase or decrease, change or stay the same?

Performance management (PM) uses scientific methods to change behavior. At first, a scientific method for managing behavior may not sound practical for line supervisors and managers, but in reality, it is the *most* practical way to manage people.

Using scientific methods to manage behavior includes precise specification of what we want to improve, the development of a baseline of current performance against which we can measure progress, and then a precise intervention and the evaluation of its impact on performance. This is no more than we would ask from any change in any other business process. As Sherman Roberts, a former colleague at the John F. Kennedy School of Management, says, "The best way to run an organization is also the best way to treat people."

2

Management by Common Sense Is Not Management at All

She knows what her responsibilities are but she just can't seem to get the job done—she has absolutely no common sense.

Most of our organizational problems can be solved by applying a little common sense.

You'll catch on, it's just common sense.

If you had any common sense at all, you would have known that wouldn't work.

I'm on a crusade to stamp out the use of common sense in business. Contrary to popular belief, there isn't too *little* common sense in business—there's too much.

Webster defines common sense as "the unreflective opinions of ordinary people." Can organizations survive on management strategies based on the *unreflective* opinions of its leaders? No! Unreflective opinions are based on unanalyzed experience. One of my favorite Benjamin Franklin quotes is: "Experience keeps a dear school, and fools will learn in no other."

A more modern equivalent was stated by W. Edwards Deming, the well-known quality guru. He said: "Experience teaches us nothing. If experience teaches us something, why are we in such a mess?"

If not common sense and not experience, then what? I think Deming would say that *systematic, data-based experience* can teach us a lot. The alternative to commonsense knowledge is scientific knowledge.

Commonsense Versus Scientific Knowledge

1. *Commonsense knowledge is acquired in ordinary business and living, while scientific knowledge must be pursued deliberately and systematically.* No special effort is required to obtain common sense. As a matter of fact, you can't stop it. It occurs just from the fact that we are alive. No wonder it's so plentiful. However, scientific knowledge requires a special effort to acquire.

2. *Commonsense knowledge is individual; scientific knowledge is universal.* The biggest problem with so-called common sense is that it is not really common at all. It's drawn from personal experience and, as such, is as different as our lives. When someone asks, "Why didn't you use your common sense?" he or she is really asking, "Why didn't you do what I would have done?" The fact is that when you use your common sense, you always do what makes sense to *you based on your experience.* Contrary to a popular TV show, there is no such place as a "no-spin zone." We cannot just walk away from our experiences. Hopefully, science will provide a corrective for bad experiences. Scientific knowledge goes beyond individual experiences to look for that which is applicable across all situations.

3. *Commonsense knowledge accepts the obvious; scientific knowledge questions the obvious.* This is probably the most distinguishing characteristic of the scientific mind versus the ordinary mind. Common sense always says, "Of course," whereas science asks, "Why?" In other words, the commonsense person always has an answer. Before science entered the picture, common sense told people that the sun came up, the stars came out at night, and the Earth was flat. Science eventually taught us

that none of these things were true even though for centuries people conducted their affairs according to these common beliefs. The scientist *begins* his or her search for the truth with the commonsense answer.

4. *Commonsense knowledge is vague; scientific knowledge is precise.* As a sports fan, one of my pet peeves is the way sportscasters inanely explain player motivation. When a player outperforms another on a play, for instance, the announcer says something like, "This player wanted it more than the other one." What does that *mean*? How would you tell the other player to succeed next time? "You need to want it more than the other player does." When the home team is losing, many fans complain that the problem is that the athletes are paid too much. Maybe so, but their opinions don't help the coach develop a winning team. The behavior analyst would want to know precisely what actions the coach can take to cause his players to "want it more than the other guy" and create outstanding performance regardless of their pay!

5. *Common sense cannot be counted on to produce consistent results; application of scientific knowledge yields the same results every time.* This is the most compelling reason for people in business to abandon common sense and seek scientific explanations to problems involving human performance in the workplace. No scientist would accept a one-time occurrence as cause-and-effect proof. A hallmark of scientific discovery is replication. Can someone else repeat the study and get the same result? Yet businesspeople constantly adopt policies and procedures that they have seen work at another company, accepting only a commonsense explanation of why those methods worked. Then, when the methods don't work in a new setting, the businesspeople compound the error by adopting other unproven strategies that someone heard about, saw, or read about in a prestigious journal. With the fierce competition in business today, we have passed the time when we can rely on trial and error to produce a workforce capable of doing the right thing every time. A business that is slow to attain high quality, bring new products to market, and respond to changing market conditions is on the road to an early demise. We must know that what we are doing will produce the desired performance *every* time.

6. *Common sense is gained through uncontrolled experience; scientific knowledge is gained through controlled experiment.* This is probably the characteristic of science that causes the average businessperson to think that it

is unrealistic for a business to use behavioral science in everyday management. This book will show you that it is not only possible but also the most cost-effective way to manage your business. Thomas Edison required his laboratory technicians to keep a detailed record of everything they did when conducting an experiment so that they could repeat it and others in the lab could do it as well. If employees keep good records, they are often able to learn from their failures as well as their successes.

The Popularity of a Management Approach Guarantees Nothing

In Search of Excellence, by Tom Peters and Robert Waterman, was published in 1982 and sold over 3 million copies worldwide in the first four years. Although it contains some valid observations, it also stands as a good example of how people accept (and follow) strong opinions and beliefs even though they are based on nonscientific information. Since the publication of that book, Peters has become one of the business world's most influential thinkers, even though three years after *In Search of Excellence* became world renowned, *BusinessWeek* magazine revisited the so-called excellent companies highlighted in the book and found that 14 of 43 of them no longer met the author's criteria for excellence. Also, in 2001, Peters confessed that the authors faked the data on which the book was based. Today he says that he didn't say that and that it was "an aggressive headline,"[1] although for the book, said by some to be the most influential business book in the 30 years since it was written, the selection of excellent companies, supposedly based on rigorous research and stringent data screens, actually was based on responses of McKinsey consultants to the question, "Who's cool?"

Ironically, some of the "cool" companies the book urged American businesses to emulate were floundering. Companies touted as the "best of the best" no longer were. In fact, several of the companies singled out for their successful management practices and commitment to customer service experienced considerable losses and underwent major reorganization after the ink was barely dry on the book. The experts failed to delve into what was going on behind the scenes at these organizations. Yet consider the impact *In Search of Excellence* had and continues to have on American and worldwide business practices. Managers around the world turned to this book to solve their management problems. Organizations spent millions of dollars to model their divisions and plants after those remarkably successful companies examined in the book. Yet, if the 14 of the 43 "cool" companies that no longer met the criteria really knew what they were doing to be successful, why would they abandon their own successful methods? Throughout history, popular practices have been found to be wrong. Think Galileo, Columbus, Newton, and many others who, despite criticism of their ideas from popular scientists and writers of the day, persisted to make discoveries that turned out to be world changing in their impact.

If It Ain't Broke, Find Out Why

An orthopedic surgeon was treating a patient for knee pain. The patient felt the pain periodically after participating in various sports activities. The doctor examined the man and could not find a specific cause for the pain. He prescribed some anti-inflammatory medicine, some antibiotics, and some painkillers. Then he wrapped the knee and told the patient to stay off it for a couple of days. Within a few days, the pain was gone.

At his next checkup, the patient said, "I'm completely cured. Doctor, you don't know how you have helped me." And the patient was right. The doctor hadn't a clue about which one of his treatments had ended the pain. Was it staying off the leg? The anti-inflammatory medicine? The antibiotics? The wrap? Perhaps even the painkillers helped. Or maybe it was a combination of everything he prescribed.

Would the pain have gone away on its own without the intervention of the doctor? Who knows? Certainly not the doctor or the patient. All they know is that the pain is gone, and to them, that's all that matters. Perhaps in a situation such as this, not knowing the exact reason the pain dissipated is unimportant. However, what if some of the treatment has masked the symptoms of a serious disease? What if the pain returns and is even more intense?

Not knowing why things get better or worse is always a problem for a business. If it gets better "for no reason," later it will probably get worse "for no reason."

Let's look at a simple example of a computer operator who is having trouble advancing to the next screen. The computer screen has locked. The operator pounds and pounds on the keyboard, hitting virtually every key until the screen advances. The operator is happy to have arrived at the next screen, but he hasn't learned how to get there the next time, let alone with grace or ease.

The next time the computer locks up, undoubtedly the operator will pound away until the screen advances again. He has no idea which key or sequence of keys unlocks the computer. By pushing keys, the operator hopes that eventually the correct screen will appear. How efficient is this? Not only is the performer not efficient, but the computer may be damaged in the process. More important, there may be a problem with the machine that, if repaired now, might save a lot of frustration as well as lost time and data in the future.

The point is, it's not enough to know that something works. It is vitally important to know *why* it works. For example, if your company is performing well and you think it's because you have an annual profit-sharing plan, you may be in for a surprise when suddenly you lose a big customer because of poor customer service. What happened? Did the profit-sharing plan quit working, or could it be that it never had anything to do with performance in the first place? The following story illustrates the pitfalls of "popular solutions."

The Guru

There once was an Indian chicken farmer who lived on the outskirts of Bombay.[2] For years, he scratched out a reasonable living from raising his chickens and selling both chickens and eggs.

One morning, when he went to feed his flock, he noticed several dead chickens. Not knowing what to do, he packed his bags and made a long trek into the Himalayas, climbed a mountain, and found a guru.

"Oh, guru," he moaned, "I am a poor chicken farmer. The other morning I discovered several dead chickens. What should I do?"

"What do you feed them?" asked the guru.

"Wheat. I feed them wheat."

"That is your problem, my son. Corn! Feed them corn."

The man paid his tribute to the guru, climbed down the mountain, and journeyed home. When he arrived, he immediately changed the chickens' feed from wheat to corn. For three weeks, everything went fine. Then one morning, as he went to feed his flock, he found more dead chickens.

He packed his bags, made the trek to the Himalayas, and climbed the mountain once again. "Oh, guru!" he cried. "More of my chickens are dead!"

"How do you give them water?"

"I carved wooden bowls in which I give them water."

"Troughs! You need troughs!"

The farmer made the long journey home and built troughs. For six months, everything went along fine. Then one morning, as he went to feed his flock, he found more dead chickens. So, again, he made the trek to the guru. "Oh, guru!" he cried. "More of my chickens are dead!"

"How do you house them?"

"I built a wooden shack in which they live."

"Ventilation! They need more ventilation!"

Back home, the farmer spent a small fortune putting a new ventilation system in his coop. For a year, everything went well. Then, one morning, he went out to discover that *all* his chickens were dead.

Beside himself with grief, he packed his bags and again made his way to the mountain. "Oh, guru!" he wailed. "All my chickens are dead!"

"That's a shame," replied the guru. "I had a lot more solutions."

There Are More Wrong Answers than Right Ones

Of all the many solutions that are proposed for solving the problems of business and industry today, how do you know what is right?

"Form self-directed teams."

"Empower the workforce."

"Encourage participation."

"Change the culture."

"Create a learning organization."

"Set up a gainsharing program."

"Use the seven habits of effective people."

And so it goes. These are only a few of the many answers that organizations are being told will make the workforce more effective. Large numbers of companies, like the guru, are blindly throwing darts at the wall, hoping to hit the bull's-eye or even the target!

The guru never systematically explored why the chickens died. The farmer received no concrete proof that the chickens' problems stemmed from their feed, or their water bowls, or even their ventilation system. He trusted the guru because he always had answers. Unfortunately, they weren't the right ones.

The guru story mirrors the search for truth by American businesses today. Management experts and theorists spew practical advice that ostensibly makes sense. Many managers today are so desperate to improve their operations or "save their chickens" that they are willing to try anything to make things better, whether it has a real effect or not. They often find themselves flooded with so many new approaches and are so busy applying them to their working environment that they have no way of determining which strategies are effective and which are not.

Maybe the farmer's chickens were sick, or maybe they were old, who knows? No one took the time to find out what was going on in the chicken coop. Do you understand the cause-and-effect relationship between your performers' behaviors and the results they produce? Do you know what motivates your employees to work hard and smart and what discourages them? Understanding the principles of performance management (PM) will provide the key to improving your employees' performance, productivity, and satisfaction because they are based on science.

Notes
1. Tom Peters, "Tom Peters's True Confessions," *Fast Company*, December 2001.
2. Don Tobin, Digital Equipment, *Target Magazine*, Marlboro, Mass., March/April 1992.

3
Louder, Longer, Meaner

It would really help if you would keep this file current.

How many times do I have to tell you to update this file?

I'm getting tired of talking to you about this file!

This is the last time I'm going to tell you this.

Keep the files current or you're fired!

In most organizations, we attempt to manage performance by telling people what to do. We tell them to work harder; we tell them to work better; we tell them to work smarter. We tell them to show more initiative, be more creative, be self-directed, be empowered!

We tell them to do these things in a variety of ways. We send memos, have meetings, write policies, hold classes, and make informational and inspirational speeches.

Interestingly, when these methods don't get the desired response or level of performance we want, we tell the same people again, usually in the same ways.

Only this time we tell them a little louder, or a little longer, or perhaps a little meaner.

We send new memos around (with bolder type, capital letters, and even exclamation marks) about old memos that were ignored or have meetings to discuss why meetings don't seem to be productive. If we train people about the importance of doing it "right the first time, every time" and they don't, we bring them in and train them again. If we try to inspire them to reach for the heavens and they barely raise their hands, we make a more impassioned plea. If our first threat gets no response, we find a more severe punishment to hold over their heads.

Surprise! People Don't Do What You Tell Them to Do

People frequently don't do what they are told. If we always did what we were told, we would eat only nutritious foods, never drink too much alcohol, and exercise regularly. We would always "put the customer first, focus on quality, take initiative, and do it right the first time."

Though we know that people don't do what they are told, we run our businesses as though the performance problems caused by people who don't know what to do, or don't want to do it, or simply don't care whether they do it can be solved by finding more and better ways of telling them what to do! In other words, we blame them.

Several years ago I conducted an informal survey and discovered that managers spend approximately 85 percent of their time either telling people what to do, figuring out what to tell them to do, or deciding what to do because employees didn't do what they were told to do. I don't think that this has changed much in the intervening years.

Why Telling Alone Does Not Bring Out the Best in People

There are two ways to change behavior. Do something before the behavior occurs, or do something after the behavior occurs. In the science of behavior analysis, the technical word for what comes before a behavior is *antecedent*. The word for what comes after a behavior is *consequence*.

Antecedents set the occasion for a behavior to occur, and consequences alter the probability that the behavior will occur again. If you are to create an organization that consistently brings out the best in people, it is critical that you understand the specific role each of these elements plays in generating performance.

Because antecedents always come *before* the behavior of interest, I refer to them as *setting events*. In other words, an antecedent sets the stage for a behavior to occur; it does *not cause* the behavior to occur. Seeing a stop sign at the corner does not cause drivers to take action to stop the car because many people who see the sign do not stop.

Consequences follow the behavior and alter the probability that the behavior will recur. That is, the consequence causes the behavior to occur more or less often in the future. While this sounds elementary, it is frequently violated in managing organizational performance.

Antecedents have limited control over behavior. *An effective antecedent gets a behavior to occur once.* It is the role of a consequence to get it to occur again.

Business success depends on getting lasting, consistent performance. Yet, as I've just described, business invests heavily in antecedent activity such as memos, training, policies, mission statements, slogans, posters, and buttons. Because antecedents get the behavior to occur once or a few times, it's apparent why businesses must continually repeat their messages. The antecedents are working, just as antecedents always do.

Effective antecedents are necessary to initiate performance but are *not sufficient to sustain performance.* Because of their preoccupation with various antecedent events, businesses waste an enormous amount of time and money in very inefficient and costly activities.

A Place for Antecedents

There are some valuable uses for antecedents. For example, we are all familiar with marketing's use of antecedents: ads, commercials, attractive packaging, sales, Internet ads, and so on. The task of marketing is to get consumers to shop on the Internet, come into the store, take a sample, or try the product "just one time."

Marketers recognize the inefficiency of influencing behavior by using only antecedents. In fact, they plan for it.

Direct mail using snail mail or Internet advertising, for example, is considered a very effective way to sell some products and services. A company advertises a three-day seminar for $1,000 and sends out 10,000 pieces of mail. To those not acquainted with this method of selling, you might be surprised to know that the company will be happy if the direct-mail campaign convinces a minimum of 20 people to attend the seminar.

This practice is considered effective because the organization sponsoring the seminar builds the inefficiency of the antecedent (8 responses per 1,000 pieces of mail and 2 attendees per 1,000) into the price of the seminar.

In day-to-day management, if only 8 employees in 1,000 respond to what we tell them, we have a major problem. Do you think we can overcome that problem by delivering the message 125 times so that everyone will finally respond? Of course that's ridiculous, but it is not far removed from actual practice.

One way to get people to continue to respond to antecedents is to continually change the antecedents. Novel antecedents are more effective than doing the same thing over and over. For example, *Just for Laughs*, the hidden-camera television show, and its predecessor, *Candid Camera*, were/are extremely effective at getting people to do "strange things" by confronting them with unfamiliar circumstances (antecedents). On one *Candid Camera* show, drivers approaching the bridge going from New Jersey to Delaware were met by a sign that read "Delaware Closed." People stopped. They had never heard of a state being closed. What could it possibly mean? What would happen if they ignored it? Could they be killed because of some dangerous situation in the state? Would they be arrested? Because people didn't know the consequences, they were cautious and stopped. Temporarily.

Business Has Always Been Enamored of Novel Antecedents.   A number of years ago, I interviewed employees of a furniture plant based in North Carolina. At the conclusion of the interview, I opened the floor to questions or comments. A man spoke up, "What's all this about 'Quality is the only thing'?" I could tell there was an underlying agenda to his question.

"What do you mean?" I asked.

"They have all these signs all over the plant that say, 'Quality is the only thing.' What does that mean?" he said.

I replied that I guessed it meant that quality was very important.

"If that's so, then why is it I see a chair that has a problem, and I set it off the line. It sits there all day 'til the end of the shift. My supervisor comes by and ain't got his production and says, 'What's wrong with that one?' I show him.

"He looks at it and says, 'Put it back. It'll run. Anyway, they'll probably catch it in the next department.' If he don't care, I don't care. I put it back on the line."

What they should have had on the signs was "Quality is our most important slogan."

Many organizations have started using such words as *associate* and *colleague* rather than *worker* and *employee* to try to cause some change in behavior. However, a person who is treated like just another pair of hands feels no different and will behave no differently just because he or she is suddenly called "associate."

Cigarette warnings are a classic example of dealing with problems through antecedent activity. Years ago, Congress debated the need for a warning on cigarettes to advise smokers of the health hazards of continuing to smoke. The debate centered first on whether to put a warning on the pack and then on what it should say. Some readers may remember that the first message said, "Warning—the Surgeon General has determined that smoking *may* be dangerous to your health."

This had little impact. Subsequently, after much debate and many tax dollars, it was decided that the problem was the verb "may be." The new warning read, "Warning—the Surgeon General has determined that smoking *is* dangerous to your health." How many smokers do you know who pulled out their cigarettes to light up, looked at the new warning, and said, "Whoa! Do you know these things are dangerous? I'm gonna stop." (The government doesn't know one either.) So, true to form, Congress debated again and decided that it needed several different warnings defining the specific dangers. This was more effective, right? Of course not. There is no evidence that any of these printed warnings had any effect on smokers whatsoever.

Some people might point to the fact that cigarette smoking has declined rather dramatically from former levels. That's certainly true, but I suggest that what really changed smoking behavior was the change of consequences: no smoking on planes, in restaurants, or in public buildings. These changes and the negative social reaction to people who smoke have had more impact on smoking behavior than all the warnings ever printed.

The U.S. government assumes that people read and respond to warnings. Companies are required to warn customers of side effects of drugs. Paper coffee cups have warnings telling customers that the contents are hot. Ladders have warnings that tell customers that you can be seriously hurt if you fall off. The consequence to a company of not warning customers of the dangers is a lawsuit. Courts usually side with the companies that warn the customer of danger.

Recently, I read a newspaper article with the title, "Alcohol and Pregnancy: Warnings Don't Work." I thought, *finally someone is getting the message about the weak effect of antecedents on behavior.* I was disappointed to learn that the article's author merely pointed out that the warnings were difficult to read. She then stated that the warning should be larger and more conspicuous. When will we ever learn?

The only thing that makes an antecedent effective is its consistent pairing with a consequence. People have to experience the pairing more than once or twice before they will respond reliably to the antecedent time and time again.

No matter how attractive or frightening an antecedent is, it will have a long-lasting effect only if it is consistently paired with a consequence that is meaningful to the person involved.

For example, a sign that says "Handicapped parking only—Violators will be fined" is often ignored because the spaces are conveniently located for everyone, the parking lots are usually not well patrolled, and fines are rarely given for parking in a handicapped space.

However, signs that reliably predict consequences are reliably followed. Put a sign on a fence surrounding a generator that reads "Danger—High Voltage" and the fence will likely not be touched—if the person can read and sees the sign. Most people learn early that electricity hurts *every time you touch it.*

This is the good news and bad news about antecedents. Antecedents can be found to get a behavior to occur one time. The bad news is that they get the behavior to occur only once or a few times. Because very few managers understand how or why antecedents work or the need to pair them with the right consequences, they continue to search for new antecedents.

Threat as Antecedent—Not Consequence

The search for more effective antecedents unfortunately has led many supervisors and managers to use threats to get their people to perform. Most people think of a threat as a consequence because it implies punishment. But because the threat comes *before* the behavior you want, it is only an antecedent. For example, if you say, "Clean up this area by four o'clock or you'll have to stay and finish it after everyone else has gone," the person may begin to clean up the area. However, if the person knows you never follow through on such threats, he or she may not finish cleaning before leaving or may not clean thoroughly. The threat is only an antecedent. The threat only sets the stage for the cleaning to begin.

Antecedents Get Us Going—Consequences Keep Us Going.   A number of years ago, when I worked more actively as a management consultant, I was asked to help a supervisor solve a quality problem on his shift. As I approached his work area, I saw that his manager had him cornered. The manager's face was red, his voice was loud, and his language was abusive as he shook his finger in the supervisor's face. Witnessing this made me uncomfortable because, after the manager left, I had to talk to the supervisor about using positive reinforcement to improve quality.

When the manager left, I said, "Wow, he got off to a rough start this morning, didn't he?" The supervisor replied, "Aw, don't pay him no mind. That's the way he is. If I'd been fired every time he told me I was going to be fired, I wouldn't work here a week. He threatens to fire me at least once a week."

Taking that kind of abuse was a part of the job as he saw it. It meant nothing. He had learned to ignore it.

Without consequences, threats are so much hot air. In the same way, promises of positive consequences, without follow-through, mean nothing. Without reinforcement, no behavior can survive for long.

Most managers are convinced that the basic problem is poor communication. Ultimately, the search for effective antecedents is never ending and futile. Louder, longer, and meaner antecedents will not give us the consistent performance we require from our workforce.

PART 2

The Astonishing Power of Positive Reinforcement

4
Behavior Is a Function of Its Consequences

*People do what they do because of what
happens to them when they do it.*

At the end of every working day, people leave work either more motivated to come back and do their jobs again tomorrow or less motivated as a result of what happened to them that day. Performance is about *what happens every day.*

Everything we do changes our environment in some way. When a behavior changes our environment in ways that we like, we repeat it. When our behavior changes the environment in ways we don't like, we stop. Everything we do produces a consequence for us that changes our behavior.

Technically defined, *behavioral consequences are those things and events that follow a behavior and change the probability that the behavior will be repeated in the future.* This definition allows scientists to study and predict behavior through systematic observation. However, the concept is enormously useful to the nonscientist as well. Because we can observe the impact of a particular consequence on the rate or frequency of a behavior, we can begin to understand how to influence or change any behavior.

31

Consequences change the rate or frequency of a behavior. They cause a behavior to occur either more or less often in the future. There are only four behavioral consequences. Two increase behavior and two decrease it. The two that increase behavior are called *positive reinforcement* and *negative reinforcement*. The two that decrease behavior are called *punishment* and *penalty* (Figure 4-1).

Let's say that an employee engages in 1,000 behaviors per day at work. Each is followed by a consequence that will either strengthen or weaken that behavior. A large percentage of these consequences occur naturally, and the employee gives them little thought. For example, he or she turns the key in the door to the building, pulls on the knob, and the door opens. The employee flicks the switch and the lights come on. The door opening and the lights coming on are natural consequences for these behaviors. The fact that they work causes these behaviors to be repeated under the same conditions.

Another portion of the 1,000 behaviors is followed by consequences provided by the people with whom an employee works. She smiles, says "Good morning," and receives a greeting in return. The employee shares a rumor and receives the smiles and attention of peers.

Yet another portion of the 1,000 behaviors is followed by consequences provided by supervisors and managers. The intent of many consequences provided by managers and supervisors is to do things that increase the behaviors that directly add value to the business and decrease those that interfere with value-added performance.

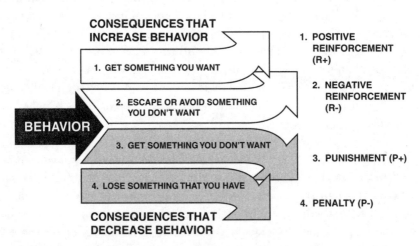

Figure 4-1 Summary of the four behavioral consequences and their effects.

As a manager, could you explain to a visitor what you are doing to make sure that the right consequences are occurring every day for the right behaviors?

Think about your organization for a moment. Are only value-added behaviors being strengthened by consequences in the work environment? Or are off-task behaviors reinforced in some manner? Is it possible that some of the behaviors you don't want to occur again are receiving consequences that actually increase the probability of those behaviors recurring?

I tell people that I can go into their organization and immediately see what is being reinforced. All I have to do is observe what people are doing. *What they do during the workday is what is being reinforced.*

Vic Dingus, former technical associate at Eastman Chemical Co., points out that *a company is always perfectly designed to produce what it is producing.* If it has quality problems, cost problems, productivity problems, or safety problems, then the behaviors associated with those undesirable outcomes are being reinforced. This is not conjecture. This is the hard, cold reality of human behavior.

This is good news because it means that all we have to do to get the performance we want is *to identify the behaviors that will produce the desirable outcomes and arrange consequences that will positively reinforce those behaviors.* In some cases where behavior is increasing risk to the performer or to colleagues, you also may need to *identify consequences that will stop them.* Often, by identifying behaviors we want and strengthening them, we make the use of punishment unnecessary or at least a rare event in the workplace.

Can we introduce and arrange consequences in such a way that tasks that are now difficult, dull, or boring become exciting, challenging, and rewarding? Is that possible? It most definitely is.

Every Consequence Every Day

In everyday affairs, all four of the behavioral consequences are at work. It is practically impossible to live a day without experiencing all of them. For example, you are talking on your cell phone and you lose your connection (*penalty*). When you tried to use a computer for the first time, you probably inadvertently deleted a document after working on it for hours (*punishment*). Now, you talk about how writing memos by hand for your assistant to type is still the best way for you to get your correspondence done. You stay late on Thursday night to revise a presentation because you know that if the first draft isn't letter perfect, the boss will chew you out (*negative reinforcement*). You bought one of your staff members a cup of coffee while he was finishing a project three days before it was due. The next project was completed a week ahead of schedule (*positive reinforcement*).

Each type of consequence has a different influence on the behavior it follows. A significant part of every manager's job is to identify the behaviors that are necessary and sufficient to accomplish the company's objectives and then to arrange for consequences that support them.

Increasing Performance via Reinforcement

The two kinds of reinforcement, positive and negative, increase behavior. Positive reinforcement causes a behavior to increase when a desired, meaningful consequence follows it. Negative reinforcement causes a behavior to increase as a means of escaping or avoiding some unpleasant consequence. It is important to know the difference because the characteristics of the performance generated by each are *very* different.

Negative reinforcement generates enough behavior to escape or avoid punishment. The improvement is usually described as "doing just enough to get by." Positive reinforcement generates more behavior than is minimally required. We call this *discretionary effort*, and its presence in the workplace is the only way an organization can maximize performance.

Because reinforcement is defined as any consequence that increases performance, it always works. If performance does not increase following the delivery of a consequence, then, by definition, the consequence was not a positive reinforcer. This means that an organization that uses reinforcement effectively *will get improvement*. Put another way, if performance is not improving, reinforcement is not occurring.

Consequences That Decrease Performance

As stated previously, just as there are two consequences that increase behavior, there are two consequences that decrease behavior: *punishment* and *penalty*. Because punishment, like positive reinforcement, is defined by its effect, we can say that a particular thing or event is punishing only when we see its effect on behavior. This is a very important principle for managers. This means that a "chewing out" for poor-quality work could be a positive reinforcer, rather than a punisher as intended, if it resulted in an increase in poor-quality performance. By the same token, a "pat on the back" is actually a punisher if it causes a decrease in performance, and it's not unusual for this to be the case. For a pat on the back to be a positive reinforcer, the person has to care about what the supervisor thinks. If the employee does not like or respect the supervisor, that pat on the back is unlikely to increase performance.

Anyone in business who doesn't understand how consequences operate and vary from person to person can accidentally create problems while trying to improve performance. Without doubt, most of the punishment that goes on in the average organization is unintentional.

Most managers think that intention determines effect. That is to say, most managers think that if they intend to positively reinforce someone for good performance, then that is what they are doing. Unfortunately, this is not true. The consequence is defined as positive or negative by the performer—the person who receives it. That is to say, by his or her response.

Doing Nothing Is Doing Something to Performance

If inadvertent punishment is common, inadvertent extinction is epidemic. *Extinction* is technically defined as the withdrawal of positive reinforcement from a behavior, but it may be easier to understand this way: *the performer does something, and nothing happens.* Ignoring is probably the most common example of extinction. We know extinction is occurring when we hear people say such things as, "Nobody appreciates anything I do around here."

Most managers feel that doing nothing has no effect on performance, as in the remark, "I didn't do anything." The fact is that when managers do nothing following employee performance, they may change that performance in one of two ways: (1) they put desired effort on extinction, and (2) they open the door for some inappropriate behavior to be positively reinforced. And managers do this all the time!

If people are taking the initiative to go above and beyond what is required, then those behaviors, if they lack a favorable consequence, will stop at some point. If people are taking shortcuts in areas such as safety and quality, the naturally occurring positive consequences (saving time and effort) will cause those behaviors and activities to continue.

Management changes behavior by its action and its inaction. Let's say that you have 30 people reporting to you. How many would be problem performers? Two, maybe three? Now look at how you spend your time. Is it possible that you might spend as much or more time with the three problem performers as you do with the other 27? It happens. This indicates that you are ignoring the good performance that makes your company successful while giving your full attention to poor performance. The extinction of good performance is a common complaint of business. It sounds something like this: "People just don't have that old-fashioned work ethic anymore."

Decades of ignoring good performance have taken their toll. We have put the "work ethic" on extinction not by what we did so much as what we didn't do.

A Change of Focus

A retired maintenance superintendent was called back to a Chrysler plant to train new employees involved in the startup manufacturing of a new car. He was one of several people who made a presentation to plant management about the new product and the production training process.

He introduced himself by saying, "I'm Don F. Many of you don't know me, but I retired from this plant last year. Since I retired, I've had a lot of time to think about my career here. I started as a mechanic in the maintenance department and after many years became maintenance superintendent for the entire plant. As I thought about those days since retiring, something bothered me. Of the hundreds of employees that I supervised and managed during my career here, I can remember the names of about 30 that I would classify as 'no good.'

"I can remember the names of about the same number who were 'outstanding.' That's 15 to 20 percent of everyone I managed. What really bothers me is the remaining 80 to 85 percent who came in and did their jobs every day, who were the people primarily responsible for my success in the plant, and I can't even remember their names. I hope when you retire you don't bear that burden."

Bringing out the best in people requires that *all* performers get the right consequences *every day*. Making this happen is in large part a supervisor's job. We shouldn't ignore poor performers, but if we are to have a high-performance organization, we *can't* ignore the good performers either.

The More Immediate, the Better

All four types of consequences are subject to *impact erosion*. This means the shelf life of a consequence is limited. The more immediate the consequence, the more effective it is in changing behavior. Everyone who has ever tried to change a bad habit understands this. We want to lose weight, but we eat high-fat, high-calorie foods today, vowing to change tomorrow. We vowed to start an exercise program today, but we watch our favorite TV show instead. We want to quit smoking, but first we finish that last pack of cigarettes. The immediate consequences of smoking—taste, relaxation, and stress reduction—far outweigh the delayed and uncertain consequences of better health.

Consequences that are immediate and certain are very powerful in governing behavior. For example, if, when handling caustic chemicals, performers know that a small drop on the skin will produce an immediate and painful blister, it will not be a problem to get them to wear gloves. However, performers who handle lacquer products that may cause cancer and/or possible nerve damage with prolonged exposure may not consistently wear protective gloves. Many old-timers don't wear them at all.

Reinforcers Are More Effective than Rewards

The immediacy factor explains the difference between a reinforcer and a reward. Although that difference will be examined in more detail later in this book, for now, you should remember that a small reinforcer provided immediately for a behavior has much more effect on that behavior than a larger but delayed reward.

Because a reward is usually in the future, there is always a degree of uncertainty associated with it. Those offering the reward may withdraw it or change the conditions necessary to get it. The performer might not be able to meet the conditions, could die, or otherwise may not qualify for the reward. People typically respond more predictably to small, immediate, certain consequences than they do to large, future, uncertain ones.

The consequences that cause people to do their best every day occur every day. Yet experience has shown that most organizations spend more time, energy, and money providing consequences that occur when employees get sick, retire, or die than on the ones that occur every day.

This has enormous implications for every firm. It means that bonuses, profit sharing, retirement benefits, and similar forms of compensation are future, uncertain consequences and, as such, do not bring out the best in people every day. These incentives are expected *but not sufficient* to maximize performance. Certain forms of compensation facilitate performance better than others. However, compensation alone will not do the job of maximizing performance. Only effective and frequent positive reinforcement can do that.

Management Myth: People Resist Change

Another important implication of the effect of consequences on behavior involves the critical element of change. We are continually bombarded with rhetoric about the urgency and acceleration of change in today's "fast-paced business world." We are told that people naturally resist change. This has become a major concern for most businesses, and many have invested millions learning how to "manage change."

The fact is that *people don't resist change if the change provides immediate positive consequences for them.* Nobody resists change when the immediate consequences favor it. "Do it this way, and you won't hurt your fingers." "Hold the light this way, and you will be able to see it better." "Move your right hand this way, and you will be able to hit the golf ball straight." If the correct behavior follows these instructions and positive consequences occur, we will not have a difficult time getting people to accept change in those situations. It is only in situations where the immediate consequences of change are punishing or where the new behavior is not immediately reinforced that we run into trouble.

Almost every corporate initiative affects performers negatively at first. While the performers may understand that there are long-term benefits to the company and to the performers personally, the immediate consequences of doing things differently are usually negative. New behaviors require extra effort to learn, result in increased mistakes, cause the performers to fall behind in their other work, and create stress because people fear they won't be able to learn or perform as well under new conditions.

To make change a positive experience, we need to be less concerned with managing the change and much more attentive to managing the consequences associated with change.

Everybody's Behavior Makes Sense to Them

As unbelievable as it may sometimes seem, every person's behavior makes sense to him or her. This is so because everyone is reinforced in different ways. Initially, what is reinforcing to another person may not be obvious to us, but if we look a little deeper, we can discover the consequences that maintain almost any behavior.

One of my associates, Dick Cross, once witnessed some of this seemingly inexplicable behavior when a woman he was dating asked him for help after she received a promotion to department manager in a federal government office in North Carolina. She soon discovered that her job wouldn't be an easy one. The office she had inherited had a statewide reputation for poor performance. When each office received monthly ratings on a variety of performance measures, her new department invariably ranked at or near the bottom. At this point she quickly asked Dick for help.

The two spent several weekends and evenings developing individual and group measures. Their implementation involved graphing individual and group performance and displaying office results daily, developing reinforcement plans, and celebrating improvement. In a short time, the office zoomed from near the bottom to close to the top in performance ratings.

Shortly after the dramatically improved ratings came out, the office manager's boss called her and said, "I don't know what it is you're doing down there, but I want you to stop." The woman was shocked. Expecting praise, she received punishment instead! "This man must be crazy!" she thought. "Didn't he hire me to do the best possible job, to turn the office around?"

Not until several days later did she learn what had caused his unlikely reaction. Before she began her improvement efforts, her boss had spent considerable time trying to convince his boss that the only way to improve the situation in North Carolina was with more money and more people. She had accomplished the necessary improvement with neither of those organizational changes—changes that her boss anticipated would lead to his reinforcement and reward.

In retrospect, the reaction of the office manager's boss was perfectly understandable when considering the embarrassment her success caused him. His behavior was even easier for her to understand when she discovered that his pay grade was, in part, determined by the number of people in his department and the size of his budget. This is an example of an organizational structure that provides positive consequences for the wrong behaviors and results!

No-Fault Performance: Change—Not Blame

When you understand how consequences influence performance, you realize that finding fault with people for their inappropriate performance is unproductive and unfair. They are simply behaving in a manner consistent with the consequences they are receiving now and have received in the past.

The role of leaders in every organization is not to find fault or place blame but to analyze why people are behaving as they are and modify the consequences to promote the behavior they need. As I mentioned earlier, this approach to management does not overlook poor performance. Nor does it seek to use only positive reinforcement to attempt to create some type of unrealistic, utopian organization. Quite the contrary.

The management system we should create employs all the consequences appropriately and skillfully to promote the behavior that supports the organization's goals and to stop problem behaviors that interfere with accomplishing them. Managers and supervisors who can differentiate between and effectively provide all four types of consequences will quickly achieve levels of performance they may never have thought possible.

5

The ABCs of Performance Management

A Way of Seeing Things as Others See Them

In Chapter 4, I explained how apparently senseless behavior made sense to the performer because it was in some way positively reinforcing to that performer. However, as in the example of the department supervisor in the federal government, it's often difficult to understand how some things that others do could make sense to anybody.

So the first step when attempting to change the way people perform is to *understand why they are currently behaving the way they are.* We now know that people do what they do because of the consequences they experience following their actions. Therefore, it is helpful to discover what antecedents are setting the stage for the behavior to begin, and it is necessary to know what consequences are causing the behavior to continue.

The PIC/NIC Analysis is a simple method for systematically analyzing the antecedents and consequences influencing a behavior. This analytical technique will allow you to understand behavior from the other person's perspective, even when it appears to you to be unproductive, irrational, or self-defeating (Figure 5-1).

ANTECEDENT	:	BEHAVIOR	➡	CONSEQUENCE
(Setting Event)		(Performance)		(Reinforcer/Punisher)

Figure 5-1   ABC model of behavior change.

First, some definitions:

Antecedent: Something that comes before a behavior that sets the stage for the behavior or signals it to occur.

Behavior: What a person does.

Consequence: What happens to the performer as a result of the behavior.

Examples:

Antecedent	Behavior	Consequence
Your nose itches	You rub it	Stops itching
Gas gauge registers empty	Fill your empty tank	Continue your trip without worry about running out of gas
Telephone rings	You answer	Customer places large order

Once you view performance in terms of antecedent-behavior-consequence (ABC), you will be able to develop solutions to performance problems that you may never have attempted in the past.

Before you begin to analyze any performance problem, you should determine whether the problem is a motivational problem (won't do) or a skill problem (can't do). Robert Mager popularized this important problem-solving step in his book *Analyzing Performance Problems*. Mager suggested imagining whether the person would do what you ask if threatened with bodily harm if it is not done. If he or she doesn't do it under these conditions, the previous lack of performance is most likely a training problem. If the performer does it then (and wasn't doing it before), it is a motivational problem.

Of course, we can't practice this technique, but we can realize that most of the problems we face in day-to-day management *are* motivational problems. Nevertheless, we should always make the "won't do/can't do" determination before proceeding. One hint: if the person has done the behavior correctly in the recent past but is no longer doing it or is doing it poorly, it's probably a motivational problem.

Motivational problems in the context of this book include all situations where the performer knows the correct behavior, can perform the correct behavior, but doesn't do it. Sometimes people may be able to do what is required but don't know that it is time to do it. Or they may be doing the correct behavior but not at the correct rate. And, of course, sometimes they may know that it's the right time and can perform at the correct rate but choose to do nothing. People always have the choice to vary their performance.

Keep in mind that the applicability of this analysis doesn't stop on the shop floor. Managers and executives also perform according to the consequences they receive.

In the PIC/NIC consequences are classified on three dimensions:

1. *Positive or negative.* This dimension answers the question, "Is the performer likely to experience the consequence as positive or negative?"
2. *Immediate or future.* Here we want to know, "Does the consequence occur as the behavior is happening, immediately thereafter, or after some time has passed in the future?"
3. *Certain or uncertain.* This dimension expresses the probability that the performer will actually experience the consequence.

Let's look at an example. Some people don't wear seat belts. An objective analysis of this behavior shows that seat belts save lives and reduce injuries. Why, then, would a person not buckle up? Look at Figure 5-2. (In Figures 5-2 through 5-5, the designations P/N, I/F, and C/U refer to positive or negative, immediate or future, and certain or uncertain, respectively.)

What the analysis in Figure 5-2 tells us is that

1. There are many antecedents that set the stage for *not buckling up seat belts.*
2. Although there are many serious negative consequences associated with *not buckling up seat belts*, those consequences tend to be in the future, they are uncertain to occur, or both.
3. The positive consequences of *not buckling up seat belts*, such as "saves time," "freedom to move," and "doesn't wrinkle clothes," are small but immediate and certain.

Let's look at what might happen if this same person who doesn't wear a seat belt actually puts one on, as shown in Figure 5-3.

Antecedents	Consequences	P/N	I/F	C/U
Think they don't work	Death	N	F	U
Can't reach easily	Injury	N	F	U
Just going on short trip	Get ticket	N	F	U
	Saves time	P	I	C
In a hurry	Easier	P	I	C
Accident has never happened to me	Freedom to move in seat	P	I	C
	Won't be trapped by belt	P	I	C
	Clothes won't get wrinkled by belt	P	I	C

Figure 5-2   Problem behavior: Not buckling up seat belt.

Desired Behavior: Buckling Up Seat Belt

Antecedents	Consequences	P/N	I/F	C/U
Saw accident	Less chance of dying in accident	P	F	U
Got a ticket				
Passenger asked to put it on	Less chance of injury	P	F	U
	Took more time to get started	N	I	C
Saw police officer	Restricted movement	N	I	C
	Wrinkling clothes	N	I	C
	Felt uncomfortable	N	I	C

Figure 5-3   Desired behavior: Buckling up seat belt.

If our non-seat-belt wearer was to put on the belt, he or she would find that

1. The positive consequences tend to be future and uncertain.
2. The negative consequences are immediate and certain.

This analysis points out the difficulty in changing any behavior. The present behavior or habit (usually what you don't want) is receiving positive, immediate, and certain consequences (PICs), and the desired behavior gets negative, immediate, and certain consequences (NICs). So what we want this performer to do (wear a seat belt when riding in a car) is associated with immediate punishment and the possibility of future benefits. What we don't want this performer to do (ride in a car without wearing a seat belt) is associated with immediate positive reinforcement and the uncertain possibility of some future, possibly serious injury.

If you put any problem behavior through this analysis, it will essentially come out the same, whether the problem is at home, at work, or at play. What you will most certainly find is PICs for the problem behavior and NICs for the desired behavior. Let's take a look at a common work-related behavior problem, as shown in Figure 5-4.

Antecedents	Consequences	P/N	I/F	C/U
Peers do it that way	Easier to do	P	I	C
No feedback on individual errors	Takes less time	P	I	C
	Every claim processed is accepted	P	I	C
Performance appraisal has quantity category	Get praised by boss for meeting quantity goal	P	I	U
Office has quantity goals and graphs on wall	Customers are unhappy with company and cancel policy	N	F	U
Got chewed out for missing quantity goal				

Figure 5-4 Undesired behavior: Processing claims without attention to quality.

Antecedents	Consequences	P/N	I/F	C/U
Signs in office (Quality is key)	Takes more time	N	I	C
	Less time to socialize	N	I	C
Boss said "Be careful"	Requires more effort	N	I	C
Performance appraisal has quality as a category	Requires more concentration	N	I	C
	Good appraisal	P	F	U
Got chewed out for mistakes from last month	Might get a raise	P	F	U
Received training	Missed quality goal	N	F	U

Figure 5-5   Desired behavior: Process all claims accurately.

As you can see, the undesired behavior (processing claims fast, without concern for quality) is met with a number of naturally occurring PICs. There are even several provided *by management* that actually conflict with the consequences that management professes to support.

The desired behavior, processing claims accurately (shown in Figure 5-5), results in a number of NICs, and the only positive consequences are future and uncertain. In this case, it will be difficult to encourage this employee to change behavior.

When doing a PICNIC Analysis, it is important to understand that the classification of a single consequence may be unimportant. What *is* important is the *pattern* of PICs and NICs you can identify. You will quickly find out that some consequences can be accurately classified only after much study. Because we are trying to look at the problem from the other person's perspective, we can be 100 percent accurate only if we can read minds, which I confess I can't.

However, we can identify patterns that will enable us to rearrange consequences so that they are more favorable for the desired behavior. It has often been stated that "The ability to do a good ABC analysis is an indirect measure of empathy."

Building Trust

By now, you should begin to see that understanding and managing consequences are the most effective ways to improve performance. In the chapters that follow, I will explain how to create, arrange, and provide effective consequences in the workplace. However, before we go on, let me write a few words about trust.

Understanding why people behave the way they do and then arranging consequences to influence that behavior are only the beginning. The major factor in determining whether you can change behavior in the long term depends on the extent to which you can consistently pair *antecedents with consequences*. We call this dependable pairing of antecedents with consequences *trust*. In other words, to be trusted, all you have to do (*consequence*) is do what you say you are going to do (*antecedent*).

An old saying goes: "After all is said and done, more is said than done." This is not only the way some managers and supervisors behave but also a characteristic of many companies as well. If we tell employees that doing something a particular way will be easier for them and it's not, we've slightly eroded their trust. If we tell someone that if she works hard she will be better off, and she is not, we lose more credibility. If we tell people that they will be promoted, get a raise, get a transfer, head up a project, or be on a team and these things do not come to pass, we destroy trust.

Organizations often think that poor communication is the biggest barrier to organizational effectiveness. In reality, some organizations communicate too much rather than too little. If the organization is communicating things that don't happen, for whatever reasons, employee trust of upper management will be eroded and eventually become nonexistent. More communication is not better if we communicate things that don't happen. Whatever we communicate, we have to make sure that it happens.

When people say we don't communicate, they aren't saying that we don't talk. They are saying that after we talk, nothing changes. I've chosen to make this point now because you are about to learn how to use performance management skills to manage your business and to bring out the best in people. If you view these principles and techniques as tools to manipulate behavior in your favor without requiring you to use them in absolute good faith, you will fail.

Once trust is established, people will give you the benefit of the doubt if you make a mistake. If you are not trusted, they will not believe you even when you tell the truth.

6

The High Price of Negative Reinforcement

*Be careful that victories do not carry
the seeds of future defeats.*
— *Bits & Pieces Magazine*

We are all well aware of the many efforts being made to improve the way we manage the workplace today: employee participation, teams, engagement, and so on. With this swirl of activity, one would think that positive reinforcement has become the dominant way that organizations are managed. Unfortunately, such is not the case.

In my many visits to organizations of all kinds, I can tell you without a doubt that negative reinforcement is still the dominant management style. As a matter of fact, Robert Levering and Milton Moskowitz, in their 1988 edition of the national bestseller, *The 100 Best Companies to Work for in America*, make the following comment:

> Found in all parts of the country and in all types of industry, they [the 100 best companies] represent a signal departure from the hierarchical, dictatorial workplace that has prevailed for so long in

American business. But they are also exceptional rather than typical. They stand out because they are so different. Most companies still offer dreadful work environments.

Let me give you an example where an organizational practice thought to be positive became instead a very negative experience. Several years ago a man approached me during a break in one of my seminars and said, "Our company has gone crazy over teams. You can't do anything by yourself anymore. I was on a team with eight other chemical engineers for 18 months. It was the worst experience of my industrial life." (The team was a cross-functional team working on a quality problem at a large industrial site.)

He continued, "There was not one time during the entire 18 months that all nine of us agreed on anything! We fought like cats and dogs! It seemed that everybody was out for their own interests without regard for the rest of the team. I never was so happy as when we completed our final report and disbanded the team! About two weeks later we all got a note from our boss's boss thanking us for our 'teamwork and cooperation.'"

I won't tell you what he said his boss could do with the memo because it is not polite, but he continued, "That's just the problem around here. Nobody at the top has the slightest idea what we have to put up with at the bottom. If he thinks he can just sit up there and dash us off a note and think he's got us in his hip pocket, he's got another thought coming!"

If I were to talk to the boss's boss about positive reinforcement, he would tell me that he is already doing it. He would probably pull out copies of the memos he sent to each team member to illustrate his claim.

What happened here? Aren't teams one way to create a positive work environment? Maybe, but in this case, was there any positive reinforcement at work? Well, obviously, the work itself was not reinforcing, the team members did not reinforce each other, and the boss's boss was insincere and even inaccurate with his note, so he provided no positive reinforcement. In other words, little positive reinforcement was available for the team members' behaviors from team members or from management.

So why did the team members labor for 18 months on the project? Because they had to. The engineer in this example and millions like him are behaving in new ways not because they want to but because they have to. Doing things because you have to do them is a sure sign that negative reinforcement is the consequence at work.

From the foregoing description, it is obvious that the boss thinks he is managing by positive reinforcement but is using negative reinforcement instead. Of course, no one will tell him, so he will probably continue sending well-meaning but meaningless memos.

This is not an uncommon problem. While most managers these days agree that it is better to manage with positive reinforcement than with negative reinforcement, there are very few who understand the difference. Programmatic attempts at positive management techniques demonstrate this lack of understanding. Just because you have initiatives such as teams, participation, and engagement does not mean that you are getting results through positive reinforcement. In fact, if these initiatives are being managed in the same way work was managed before they were begun, negative reinforcement is undoubtedly the dominant consequence.

Positive or Negative Reinforcement: What Difference Does It Make?

There are only two ways to get organizational results. One is through positive reinforcement, and the other is through negative reinforcement. If both get results, why should we care?

I believe that everybody would agree that if both positive and negative reinforcement got exactly the same results, it would still be better to use positive reinforcement. Why? First of all, people like positive reinforcement better. It produces a less stressful workplace. For this reason alone, positive reinforcement should be preferred.

However, there is an even more compelling business reason. *Positive reinforcement maximizes performance, while negative reinforcement gets a level of performance that is just enough to get by*—just enough to escape or avoid some unpleasant consequence. For example, a team brings a tough project in on time, but everyone on the team knows they could have done the job in a shorter period of time.

Because both kinds of reinforcement get improvement, it is important for management to know whether the improvement has been accomplished through positive or negative reinforcement. You see, if you are getting results with negative reinforcement, you are missing the substantially greater results you could be getting if positive reinforcement were the consequence at work.

How Can You Know?

What are the indications that you are using negative reinforcement when you think you are using positive reinforcement? When I walk into a workplace, there are several clues I look for that tell me which consequence is driving performance. Before going into each one in detail, let's examine the way negative reinforcement works to improve performance.

Let's say that because of a recent job change, someone is assigned to you who is performing very poorly. Let's also say that you know that the person is capable of good performance because that individual has performed much better in the past, but for a variety of reasons this person's performance has dropped below satisfactory. Because the person has worked for the company for a long time, the previous supervisor tolerated the poor performance. Now, because of increased competitive pressures, everyone has to improve, so you cannot tolerate this individual's substandard performance.

You go to the employee and say, "Seventy parts per hour is entirely unsatisfactory, and if you can't get performance up to 100 parts per hour by 30 days from today, I will have to terminate you." Now let's say that the person believes you because she knows that you have terminated others in the past. In other words, the person "is motivated" to change her performance to avoid a very unpleasant consequence—termination. When will this employee get to the goal? Will it happen on day one? If you understand how consequences work, you know that it won't. Why not?

Under negative reinforcement, *deadlines give people permission to wait.* By setting the goal 30 days away, you have told the person that it's okay to wait until the end of that time to get to the goal. This may not be what you meant, but if the person did wait and got to goal level on the last day, she would have avoided being fired under the conditions that you stated. Figure 6-1 shows graphically what this performance looks like.

Under these conditions, performance will get to goal only in the last few days of the established time period. Look at this situation from the employee's viewpoint. If she gets to goal in the first few days of the month, the only thing that she will get is to keep her job—the same consequence that would transpire by waiting until the last day. In some cases, people fear that if they get to the goal too early, someone will raise it even higher. Under those conditions, most people will wait.

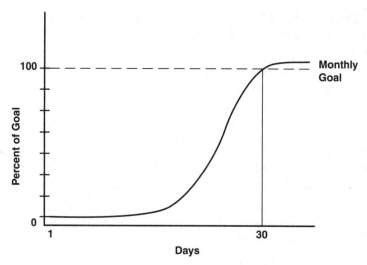

Figure 6-1   J curve performance.

Goal attainment gives people permission to stop. Now let's suppose that this "problem performer" gets to 100 parts per hour. What will she do now? She will probably hover around 100. The individual knows that even if she can do more, it's best to wait because before long the goal will probably be raised anyway. If the employee holds back now, most likely it will be easier to reach the next goal.

Deming observed this goal/performance phenomenon and frequently exhorted management to eliminate goals and standards. He said that they limit performance. Could it be that setting goals actually does limit performance? Yes and no. It depends on whether the goal is a negative reinforcer or an antecedent for positive reinforcement.

To summarize, performance motivated by negative reinforcement will tend to increase only at the last minute and then only to the "just enough to get by" level.

Five Easy Clues That Indicate That Negative Reinforcement Is Present

Because both positive reinforcement and negative reinforcement result in improvement, the following indicators constitute a checklist for you to use to see if performance in your company or department is being driven by positive or negative reinforcement:

1. *The J curve.* If performance shows a sharp rise just before a deadline, suspect negative reinforcement. If people are always scrambling at the last minute and working late and overtime to meet a deadline, check one for negative reinforcement.

2. *Negative talk.* If you hear people saying such things as, "I hate this place," you don't have to look any further for your answer to the kind of motivation that's present. However, more subtle negative talk probably will be the more common indicator. You may hear comments like

"We work under a lot of pressure here."

"I've got too much on my plate."

"They expect too much."

"That's too hard."

"Why are we always the ones? Why not ask them?"

"That's not my job."

Management may say things like

"That's what they are paid for."

"They oughta want to."

"It's their job. It's their responsibility."

"It's their fault."

Negative reinforcement produces negative talk. Positive reinforcement produces positive talk like

"Let us go first."

"We can do it."

"Let me try."

"Is there anything I can do to help?"

Check one for negative reinforcement if you hear frequent negative talk.

3. *Performance goes flat after reaching goal.* The only way this would occur with positive reinforcement is if the goal represents the highest performance possible. In practically every case where you have significant improvement to get to goal and then improvement stops, you can be fairly sure that it was attained through negative reinforcement.

   The use of *stretch goals* is also an indicator of negative reinforcement. I believe that stretch goals came about because managers noticed that unless they set additional goals, performance improvement stopped when the first goal was attained. By setting goals beyond the actual requirement, they were initially able to get more improvement. Stretch goals are used extensively, and I have unintentionally alienated a fair number of managers by criticizing their use of them. However, if performance is driven by negative reinforcement, I cannot recommend stretch goals. See: *OOPs.*[1]

   Another attempt at making goal setting more positive is to involve the performers in the development of their own goals. But even using performer participation to set goals does not guarantee that you are using positive reinforcement to attain them. Performers may set a high goal because they have experienced negative consequences when they set lower ones in the past. Setting a high goal, even if it is unreachable, may avoid a negative comment or reaction from the boss.

4. *There is no plan for positive reinforcement.* If there is no plan to celebrate the achievement of a specific goal or the successful completion of an important project, the only consequence for completion is to start work on something else. However, when the successful completion of some important task is an antecedent for positive reinforcement, people want to get started on another task. If planning a celebration for achievement is not part of your planning and goal-setting process, and celebrations do not actually take place, you can probably put another check in the negative-reinforcement column.

5. *You remove a performance requirement, and performance drops.* For example, if you announce to your work group or team that their involvement on a quality-improvement team was purely voluntary and they stopped participating, you can bet that they were doing it only because they felt that they had to do it.

Years ago, when I was consulting with the public schools, I would ask the classroom teacher to give the students an assignment and leave the room. When the teacher left, if the students stopped working and started talking, walking about the room, putting on makeup, throwing spitballs and erasers, or using cell phones and playing iTunes videos on their iPads, it indicated to me that they were studying only because they had to. If the students continued to study after the teacher left, it tended to indicate that they were studying because they wanted to. That is, the teacher had made the assignment positively reinforcing.

George Halas, legendary coach of the Chicago Bears football team, was asked when he was 79 years old how much longer he intended to work. He replied, "It is only work if you had rather be somewhere else." It is a sad fact that large numbers of people at work today would rather be somewhere else.

Is Negative Reinforcement Ever Appropriate?

Negative reinforcement is a common occurrence in everyone's life. We go to the dentist when we have to, we pay our taxes when we have to, we put on the brakes to avoid running into the car in front of us, we scratch when we itch, and we put up our umbrellas when the rain starts to avoid getting wet. The list is long. *Negative reinforcement serves performers well in circumstances where all that is necessary to avoid something unpleasant is to respond in a way that requires little time and effort.*

Although negative reinforcement is a frequent event in everyone's life, we need to find a way to avoid its use in the workplace simply because it will never bring out the best in employees. The only way to do that is with the use of positive reinforcement. If you remember in the beginning of this book, I mentioned that we all learn from our environment.

Therefore, when employees perform poorly it tells us more about the environment than about the performer. If we have a performer who has performed at a high level in the past and is now performing at a subpar level, we need to ask ourselves, "What is it about this environment that tells the employee that level of performance is OK?" It is certainly appropriate to ask the person if there are things in her life that are preventing her from performing at goal levels. If there are things outside work that are causing difficulties, try to refer her to the appropriate resources, and in some cases you may contact the resources and set up appointments for her. However, you must follow her performance and provide positive reinforcement for any improvement.

The essential skills supervisors, managers and executives need in today's workplace are shaping and pinpointing. If you are good at those two things, you are no doubt a good coach. In my opinion the words *boss*, *supervisor*, and *manager* will disappear from organization charts in the next 10 years in favor of the title *Coach* or some title that communicates to the employees that your job is to help them be successful. The skilled coach will find very few occasions to use negative reinforcement as a motivational tool.

Management Is No Place to Hold a Grudge. If you truly want employees to improve their performance, you have to forget the problems of the past and focus on the improved performance occurring in the present. Negative reinforcement can start a poor performer moving in the right direction, but only positive reinforcement can keep that person going. If you can't respond to performance as it is happening today, you will not be able to develop people. As Benjamin Franklin once said, "Write people's accomplishments in stone and their faults in the sand."

Negative Reinforcement and the Illusion of Control

The fact that negative reinforcement seems to work better than positive reinforcement is an illusion. It gives the illusion of saving time, money, and effort. In reality, it does none of these things. This illusion is grounded only in personal experience, not in scientific fact. Let me expose the illusion.

Negative Reinforcement and Control

Technically, managers get things done through either positive or negative reinforcement. Although most people think that they use positive reinforcement to get things done, the fact is that, most of the time, they don't.

Negative reinforcement is most easily recognized as the "do it or else" management approach. However, it is often difficult to spot today because modern negative-reinforcement methods are much more subtle than in days gone by. The picture of a red-faced supervisor yelling threats laced with obscenities used to be a daily affair that is etched in the memories of many old-timers. This scene has all but disappeared from the workplace, but negative reinforcement hasn't. Today, it is found most often in the use of stretch goals, threats of layoff, increased workloads, and the lack of positive reinforcement.

Because there are only a few businesses that have not been touched by a series of layoffs or downsizing, the threat is always there that "you could be next," no matter what your position or performance level. Under negative reinforcement, people work because they "have to," not because they "want to." Doing a "good job" is what you are expected to do, and not doing one is a cause for management intervention. Under this management style, the motivation is to avoid some negative consequence rather than to get a positive one.

Managers who use this style talk of control, authority, and accountability. They want people to take individual responsibility and be held personally accountable. These are code words and phrases for needing to use negative consequences on employees who fail to live up to their responsibilities. Of course by now you know that such methods place the blame on the employee as the source of the problem and the solution and all the supervisor needs to do is provide the negative reinforcement.

I have heard it said many times that managers are afraid they will "lose control" with positive reinforcement. The fact is that they don't have control with negative reinforcement in the first place. With negative reinforcement, you lose control of the following:

1. *You don't have control of your time.* For negative reinforcement to work at all, the threat of punishment for the wrong behavior must be imminent. That is, as long as the boss is physically present, he or she can get a certain performance. When the threat is removed by absence of this punisher, performance drops. This means that the negative-reinforcement manager must be always vigilant and present in person or by representation. Some companies have installed video cameras to monitor performers. Computer programs are set up to monitor whether computers are being used for business or personal use. Telephone bills are printed out by individual phones and by call to be sure they are being used only for business. The interesting thing about this is that all of it requires management to add considerable monitoring time to their already busy days.

Because under negative-reinforcement control you can't trust people to monitor themselves, you must do those things that guarantee that the company is getting what it is paying for. Checking up on people by holding meetings, by wandering around, by watching videotapes, or by analyzing telephone bills ties management down and eats up time. As it relates to control, the question is, Who is controlling whom? I know a sales manager who holds a sales meeting every Friday afternoon to make sure that all the salespeople work a full day on Friday. Whether they are working is an open question, but at least they are there. But guess what, so is he! The sales manager never gets a Friday afternoon off.

2. *You don't have control of your budget.* Because there is no positive reinforcement for beating your budget under negative-reinforcement control, the incentive is to spend it all. The manager thinks that he is exercising fiscal control when he monitors spending closely and applies negative consequences to any that exceeds allotted amounts. In reality, he is not being fiscally responsible if fiscally responsible means getting the best value for the dollar spent. The first time I had responsibility for a budget in my job at a hospital, I thought saving money while meeting my departmental objectives was actually a good thing. During my first year as a department manager, I actually beat my budget by a substantial amount. I was pleased until I realized that my budget for the following year was reduced by almost the same amount as the savings. What made it worse was that another department that I thought wasted money and practically always overspent its budget got an increase! It was the last time I had any savings. Need I say more?

Everybody who has done business with the government knows about the last-minute spending at the end of the fiscal year. Even though a manager in this situation seems to be in control, it is certainly illusory because money is often being spent before it needs to, and in some cases, it is spent foolishly.

3. *You don't have control of performance.* A colleague's brother worked for one of the major automobile manufacturers several years ago. He was a welder whose job was welding parts for the steering mechanism (today this job is probably done by a robot welder). He had a daily quota to meet. In actuality, he was able to meet the daily quota in about four hours. He continued to work for another hour or so but found a hiding place for the number he welded over his quota. This meant that the next day he only had to work a shorter time or he could work to build

up the number of finished pieces he had in his storage place. In any event, he only put as many pieces in production as he needed to meet his quota. He spent the rest of the shift doing nonwork activities.

A dead giveaway of negative reinforcement is when performance stops when the goal is reached. This is such a common occurrence that it has led to widespread use of *stretch goals* to let performers know that they are not through when they get to their first goal. This gives the illusion that the manager is in control when the goals are met. In reality, the performers are in control because they have typically "saved some performance for a rainy day."

Banking is a term often used in sales to describe a salesperson who reaches quota and stops turning in additional sales in that period, saving them for the next period. Although not as obvious in other work situations, it is more common than usually thought. Deming actually advised managers to "eliminate goals and standards" because he saw that they capped performance. That is, if you have a standard of 20 units per hour, the most you usually get is 20 per hour. It is not the goal and standard that cap performance, it is that they are used as negative reinforcers. With negative reinforcement you never know what people are capable of doing; you only know what they did, because at best they only give you a little more than is needed to avoid some undesirable consequence.

A plant's manufacturing department had never met the engineered standard. In labor negotiations, the company put in an incentive for meeting the standard. When workers met standard, they could quit work for the day. The workers consistently finished before noon and spent the rest of the day in the plant cafeteria reading and playing board games or cards! Because the union contract was for several years, the company was stuck with the situation for that time.

A manager of a motel, a retired Army master sergeant, could not have been more negative in his management style. When I pointed this out to the vice president of operations for the motel chain, he replied, "Gene has the best back-of-the-house cost in the company." I simply replied that I thought he was a problem, but it was the vice president's decision as to whether any action was taken. None was. The other 10 motels in the company implemented a positive-reinforcement system in their properties, and by the end of the year, Gene was on the bottom of the list. His performance had not slipped; the others had improved.

By relying on negative reinforcement as he did, there was no legal and ethical way that Gene could be more negative, and he was unable to get more performance out of his employees.

A similar situation occurred with the manager of street sales for a newspaper. When the manager's negative style was pointed out to upper management, the managers informed the consultant working with them that this man was a legend in the newspaper industry. He gave talks at annual industry meetings about how to manage street sales. He was completely dedicated to his job. As the upper managers began to see the progress other managers were making when they changed their management behavior from negative to positive, they moved him to another position at the paper. Within the next six months, street sales increased almost 30 percent.

4. *You don't have control of your feelings and your health.* Because negative reinforcement cannot occur without some degree of fear, the work environment is filled with stress. Keeping employees on their toes with negative reinforcement takes its toll on the manager as well as the employees. Short tempers, hurt feelings, and hostile interactions are a daily occurrence. The pressure created by lackluster performance, negative talk, and meeting goals just in time takes its toll, resulting in frayed nerves and stress-related illnesses. The best antidote to stress in the workplace is positive reinforcement. Positive reinforcement neutralizes most harmful stress.

Why, then, is it that the use of negative consequences is by far the more common way of getting things done in business, industry, and government? It is very simple. Mother Nature pulls a trick on us. Negative reinforcement is more likely to provide a positive, immediate, and certain consequence (PIC) for the user than is positive reinforcement. If you positively reinforce a behavior, you will have to wait until the next time there is an opportunity for that behavior to occur to see whether your positive reinforcement worked (positive, future, and uncertain [PFU]). If you use negative reinforcement, you are likely to see increased activity immediately (a PIC for the one using negative reinforcement).

This trick of nature hides the fact that when a substantial performance improvement is needed, the best and fastest way to get it is with positive reinforcement. Remember that positive reinforcement *accelerates* behavior. It is the only consequence that does. *Tough, competitive times demand positive reinforcement.*

Notes

1. Aubrey Daniels. *OOPs: 13 Management Practices that Waste Time and Money.*

7

Capturing Discretionary Effort Through Positive Reinforcement

Most people only know what happened;
only those who know this technology
know what's possible.
—HANK PENNYPACKER, PH.D.

Most American workers admit they could do a better job if they were properly motivated. In a "Public Agenda Report on Restoring America's Competitive Vitality," Yankelovich and Immerwahr (1983) reported that fewer than one out of four employees, 23 percent, said they that were performing to their full potential and capacity. The majority agreed that they could increase their effectiveness significantly. Nearly half the workforce, 44 percent, revealed that they did what is required of them and held back any extra effort. Amazingly, despite all the initiatives, articles, books, and training that have surfaced since 1983, engagement remains at essentially the same level as it was over 30 years ago.

Can you imagine what could be accomplished by our workforce if every employee worked up to his or her full potential every day? The question that every business leader should be asking is, How do we motivate people to "want to" do their best rather than doing only what they "have to"? To answer this question, you need to understand the concept of *discretionary effort.*

Discretionary effort is defined as *that level of effort people could give if they wanted to* but is beyond what is required. In other words, because discretionary effort is above and beyond what is expected, demanded, paid for, and planned for, there would be no punishment to the performers if they didn't do it. Discretionary effort is what is *possible.* In many organizations today, management is happy just to get what is *expected.*

Discretionary effort is within the power of every individual to give or withhold. All of us have "given a little extra" on many occasions, usually on projects that held some special interest for us. Most often this extra effort was expended on a project at home or in some activity that we enjoy.

The only way business can capture discretionary effort is through the effective use of positive reinforcement. As Russell Justice, retired industrial engineer at Eastman Chemicals, has said:

> *Discretionary effort is like loose change in employees' pockets. It is management's job to get them to want to spend it all every day.* Positive reinforcement is clearly the most effective way to manage any business. Nevertheless, of all the ways to manage, it is the most misunderstood and misused. When most people hear the words "positive reinforcement," they immediately think of things like "atta-boys," a pat on the back, a service plaque, a round of applause at a company meeting, or some kind of public recognition like "Employee of the Month." "Isn't that what you are talking about when you say positive reinforcement?" they ask me. My reply is always the same. "Absolutely not!" This shallow understanding of positive reinforcement is what prevents many managers from using it to motivate employees and improve performance.

What Does Positive Reinforcement Look Like?

Let me remind you of the definition of positive reinforcement. *Positive reinforcement is any consequence that follows a behavior and increases its fre-*

quency in the future. The fact is that most of what motivates us day to day are the little things that people do that make a big difference.

If you ask people if they received any positive reinforcement at work yesterday, most would say no. In fact, everybody at work gets positive reinforcement thousands of times every day. When you walk into your office and flip on the light switch, you get positively reinforced when the light comes on. When you pull open a desk drawer, your behavior is positively reinforced by the drawer opening. When you press your pen on a piece of paper and it makes a mark, you are positively reinforced for using the pen. When you call somebody's name, you get positively reinforced by that person responding. Every time I push a key on my computer and the correct letter appears on the screen, my key-press behavior is positively reinforced.

When you understand positive reinforcement in this context, you see how frequently it occurs in everyday functioning. If reinforcement were not built into these performances, the behavior would stop. If I pushed a computer key and never got the right letter on the screen or no letter appeared, I would quickly stop pressing the keys. If I flipped a light switch and the light never came on, I would quickly stop flipping the switch.

Apple Computer gets the credit for coming up with the concept of "user-friendly." This was a stroke of genius because early in the development of computers, most people were not positively reinforced for trying to use them. "User-friendly" is another word for positive reinforcement. At some level at least, the developers at Apple understood that if their computers were easier to use than their competitors' computers (more positively reinforcing to the user), their market would be greatly expanded.

The mouse, menus, and help screens are all attempts to put positive reinforcement into using a computer. These days many computer programs are so reinforcing that if you know how to turn the computer on, you can use it. The antecedent "Press any key to start" guarantees that anyone who can read will get reinforced. Let me define positive reinforcement another way.

> Positive reinforcement occurs every time a behavior produces a favorable change in the environment for the performer.

The problem with most work is that it has not been designed so that positive reinforcement occurs as a natural part of the process. For example, a clerk processing insurance claims does not get positively reinforced every time he processes a claim. Why? Because while the clerk is completing one claim, two more are added to the pile. The only natural consequence of processing the claims faster is getting more claims to process. It is easy to see why someone who has been processing claims for any period of time would lose his sense of urgency.

In tasks like these, management has to do something to put positive reinforcement into the job or people will never do their best. At Blue Cross Blue Shield of Alabama, when management engineered positive reinforcement into the claims adjudication process, performance increased almost 300 percent! Although this result is outstanding, it has been duplicated many times in many different jobs.

Kinds of Positive Reinforcement

There are two ways for positive reinforcement to occur: naturally and created. The examples of reinforcement illustrated earlier were *natural* reinforcement. Natural reinforcement occurs when the behavior automatically produces it. Pushing the button on a water fountain automatically produces reinforcement in the form of water. Natural reinforcers do not require the presence of another person.

Created reinforcement does not occur automatically but must be added by a person. A congratulatory note, praise, public acknowledgment, money, a plaque, and trophies are all forms of created reinforcement.

Social or Tangible

The two most common forms of created reinforcement are social and tangible. *Social* reinforcement is reinforcement that involves doing or saying something to another person. Social reinforcement includes symbolic reinforcement and anything that has *trophy value*. In this context, *trophy value* means that the trophy or symbolic reinforcer would have value only to the person or persons receiving it. *Tangible* reinforcement is a positive reinforcer that has *salvage value*, that is, something that would have value to someone else.

The most available form of created reinforcement is social reinforcement. You do not have to have a budget for it, you do not need permission to give it, and when it is given correctly, people never tire of it.

Tangible reinforcement should serve as a backup to social reinforcement—not a substitute for it. A client of ours knew that early attempts at positive reinforcement were in trouble when a supervisor, handing out merchandise earned with points for improved quality, told an employee, "Here's your damn toaster. Now get your butt back to work!"

I'll bet toast from that toaster never tasted good. In all likelihood, every time that employee looked at the toaster, it reminded him of somebody he hated. *All tangible reinforcers should be paired with social reinforcement.*

It's An Individual Thing.   Whether natural or created, what is reinforcing to a person is highly individualistic. Some people like mechanical things; others hate them. Some people like sports; others don't. Some people like to be with people; others like to be alone. Whatever you can name, you will find people who like it and people who don't.

This means that in order to reinforce effectively, you must first understand what people want or like to spend time or effort to obtain. Because reinforcement is an individual thing, this approach to management is the most employee focused of all the current approaches. What works with one person may not work with another. If you are looking for something that will work for everybody, stop. You won't find it. It doesn't exist.

This may sound too difficult or time-consuming, but it's not. The advantages you gain from increased performance make it well worth treating people as individuals—not to mention the improvement in interpersonal relationships that will result.

What Do They Want Anyway? Finding Reinforcers.   There are three ways of finding what is reinforcing: ask, try, and observe. Although common sense tells most people that the first thing you would do if you don't know is to ask, common sense would fail you again.

Try Something.   Usually, the best way to start positive reinforcement is to try something that you think might work. Most of the time, it will work because people generally find attempts at reinforcement to be reinforcing. If you make a mistake trying to positively reinforce, people generally will forgive you.

What do you try? You try things that others have found to be effective. Attention is usually a positive reinforcer because it shows that you are interested in what a person is doing. If you give approval for a particular action taken, it probably will be received as positive reinforcement. Most people like to be appreciated, so anything that demonstrates that you value them and their efforts likely will be reinforcing. Remember, you will know you have positively reinforced a particular behavior if you try and the behavior increases. If it doesn't, try again.

Ask.   The reason that asking should not be the first thing you do to discover what is reinforcing is that you may run into one or more of the following problems: (1) people may not know, (2) they may not want to tell you, (3) they may tell you what they think you want them to say rather than what they really want, and (4) asking may set up false expectations.

1. If you ask most people what their positive reinforcers are, they probably won't know what you are talking about. In addition, what a person thinks is a positive reinforcer may not be one. What people think they would work for and what they would actually work for may be very different.

2. Because of the way many people have been treated at work, they may be suspicious of your motives if you ask them what they like. If they have been managed with punishment and negative reinforcement, they may not trust you to use the information for their benefit.

3. In the climate of uncertainty created by reorganization and downsizing, people tend to "hold back." They may try to tell you what they think you want to hear rather than risk saying something that might label them as unambitious or unrealistic.

4. It is not unusual for managers, who think positive reinforcement is easy, to walk into a meeting and ask people what they want. This approach is very dangerous because it may set expectations that whatever is requested will be forthcoming. Obviously, all the things that people want will not be available at work, but this casual approach to identifying reinforcers may lead people to believe that they will be. When, subsequently, what they asked for does not become available, they become disappointed and even angry.

For these reasons, asking is not the first way to find reinforcers. Rather, after you have tried something, ask employees how they liked what you did. At this point they have a frame of reference against which to suggest other things that are likely to be acceptable. For example, if you bought lunch to reward some specific improvement in performance, when you ask what other things would be reinforcing, it is unlikely your employees will say "an extra week off with pay." In other words, your initial attempt will establish realistic expectations for what you can afford as positive reinforcers.

Observe.   You can discover a lot of potential reinforcers simply by observing what people spend their time doing when they have a choice. Many reinforcers also can be discovered just by talking to people or, better yet, by listening to them. Unfortunately, we are so busy telling people what we want that we have little time left over to listen to what they want.

Grandma's Law

Psychologist David Premack discovered in his research that when people are given a choice of things to do, whatever they consistently choose can be used as a reinforcer for the behaviors not chosen. His discovery is called the *Premack principle*. This has been more simply translated by Dr. Ogden Lindsley, who called it "Grandma's law."

Grandma's law states, "If you eat your vegetables, you can have dessert." Eating vegetables is a low-frequency choice for most children. Eating dessert is a high-frequency choice. When the high-frequency choice is made contingent on the low-frequency choice, children not only eat more vegetables, but they may learn over time to like them.

At work, this means that if we watch how people spend their time when they have a choice, it can be used as a reinforcer for them. If a mechanic spends most of his unassigned time repairing electric motors instead of doing something else, we can assume that repairing electric motors is a reinforcer to that mechanic. If when given a choice of leads a salesperson paid on a commission always chooses to call on large companies rather than small ones, that would tell us that the opportunity to call on a large client could be used as a reinforcer for that salesperson.

Grandma's law has some personal applications, too. In fact, it represents the best time-management technique available today. Here's how it works: make a list of all the things you need to do. Rank them from the things you most want to do or enjoy doing to the things you least like to do. *Then start working at the bottom of the list.*

If you do this, you will notice an interesting phenomenon as you complete tasks. When you start at the bottom, every time you finish a task, the next one on the list is more desirable, enjoyable, or interesting. If you start at the top, where most people start, the consequence of completing a task is that the next one is more undesirable, difficult, boring, and so on. In the latter approach, you look for an excuse to quit. In the former, you don't want to quit until all the tasks are done, and if you stop in the middle, you can't wait to get started again.

Case Study

A number of years ago, Gary Lorgan, department manager of Kodak's Image Loops and Sundries Department, put Grandma's law to the test. The Image Loops and Sundries Department produced image loops for Kodak's Ektaprint copiers.

Lorgan observed that the operators in his department enjoyed working on special work-related projects, usually team activities aimed at improving production quality and the production process. Of course, improvement in both areas was beneficial to the organization, so Lorgan and production supervisor Karyn Johnson decided to use team activities to reinforce the operators for meeting weekly production and quality standards. Lorgan explains:

> When the operators reach their weekly goal for each type of loop, we shut down production and let them work on other projects. In these small team activities, the operators, at their own initiative, develop ideas for improving the operation and break into teams of 2 to 10 people to implement them.
>
> We have had 15 or 20 improvements that have been made right on the production line as a result of the operators' team activities. Our production quotas are not easy to meet, but there have been times when we've made the goal late on Thursday and had the entire day Friday for team activities. Other times we've made goal just before the end of the shift or didn't make the weekly quota at all. There is no guarantee they will make it every week, but when they do, we turn them loose on their special interest projects.
>
> The operators thrive on the challenge. They monitor their own progress on a large 6- by 10-foot bar graph. Their graphs reflect cumulative effort, and each team has its own color to designate its contribution to production. The color-coded production measures make each team's results visible. This way, they get feedback on how they are doing and how they are contributing toward the weekly

goal. Highly visible daily feedback toward a common goal has inspired the operators to find ways to help each other eliminate unnecessary activities, for example, paperwork and testing.

They are so anxious to move on to their special projects that on three occasions, some operators have finished early and *volunteered* to continue working to make up a previous week's shortfall. They were able to get to their team activities those weeks, and they seemed to enjoy catching up. So that quality doesn't take a back seat to quantity, the operators perform random daily quality audits, graphing those results as well.

Since starting the team activities, production has gone up, but Lorgan sees this as the side benefit of Grandma's law. He is pleased with the production increase but remarks, "Our primary goal is not to increase productivity but to maintain it while emphasizing quality." Operational improvements made by the teams are the real plus for day-to-day operations. "The best thing about it is [that] the improvements are their ideas, and they feel good about it in the end."

Sources of Positive Reinforcement

As I discussed earlier, positive reinforcement surrounds us at work. As illustrated by Grandma's law, it can even come from the work itself. But it also comes from peers, supervisors and managers, and the environment.

Work-Related Reinforcement

The term *operant conditioning* was introduced by B. F. Skinner to explain the primary way in which we learn. What he meant was that a behavior that *operates* on the environment to produce a desirable effect for the person will be strengthened (i.e., it will occur more frequently in the future).

When we do things that "work," we are positively reinforced by the task itself. Things that go smoother or are easier when done a certain way typically will always be done that way. The "user-friendly" computer described earlier is a good example of work-related reinforcement. Anytime we can arrange a task so that reinforcement is automatically associated with the task, that task will more likely be repeated.

The concept of *job enrichment* was a well-intentioned attempt to put reinforcement into the work, but it generally has failed to meet that objective. Job simplification and job enlargement have met similar fates. Whether a clerk completes part of a form or all of the form makes little difference if the only consequence is that he or she has another form to complete. Whether a person on an assembly line puts the door on a car or builds the whole car makes little difference if good performance is taken for granted and poor performance is criticized. Building the complete car can be just as boring as putting on doors—after you've done it 20,000 times.

These efforts at making work more interesting have not succeeded because rearranging or changing the tasks is not (and never was) the issue. What has to be rearranged in the work process is positive reinforcement. Finding ways to put reinforcement into the work itself is a great first step and one that should be taken by every manager and supervisor. Grandma's law is worth trying. I will give some additional direction on how to make work more reinforcing later. However, even if reinforcement is built into the job, it will rarely be enough to bring out the best in people. Other sources of reinforcement must be tapped.

Peer-Related Reinforcement

Peers are the most effective source of reinforcement at work—and the most underutilized. Peers are in the best position to deliver positive and immediate reinforcement (positive, immediate, and certain consequences [PICs]) because they can observe performance more closely and more often than most supervisors and managers.

This source of reinforcement is rarely tapped by organizations. The problem is that most employees have never learned that it is a part of their responsibility to provide reinforcement to their peers. Worse, they are not reinforced by management when they do. The whole concept of teams has missed the mark on peer reinforcement and, as a result, has had little measurable success in improving organizational performance. Instead of using the proximity of peers to provide one another with positive reinforcement for work-related behaviors, organizations have focused teams on making process improvements. Process improvement is, of course, very important. However, without attention to the reinforcement of team members by team members, teams produce relatively few improvements and never achieve their potential. Often teams stay together but are a team in name only.

When peers recognize that they can and should be a major source of reinforcement for each other, improvements occur more frequently, much faster, and last much longer.

Management-Related Reinforcement

Since management has the overall responsibility for performance, it also has the responsibility for coordinating reinforcement. This is not to say that managers are responsible for providing all reinforcement. As I've noted, managers are responsible for providing the appropriate consequences for performance, and the most important consequence they can provide is positive reinforcement. But it is not practical and, in fact, it is not possible for managers and supervisors to provide all the reinforcement employees will receive. The job of management is to ensure that reinforcement occurs for the right behavior, at the necessary frequency, and from all sources available. Planning and delivering reinforcement are the two most important behaviors of supervisors and managers.

The manager who can harness the power of positive reinforcement for value-added performance will be the manager who can capture and enjoy the benefits that discretionary effort provides for the people and the company.

8

Decreasing Behavior— Intentionally or Otherwise

By now you know that if behaviors are occurring, there must be some reinforcement for them somewhere in the environment. No reinforcement equals no behavior. And you have known for a long time that the behavior that occurs is not always the behavior that you want. I have spent the last two chapters writing about how to increase and even maximize behavior. I will spend this chapter writing about how to reduce or even stop behavior.

I described the consequences that stop or reduce behavior briefly in Chapter 4. They are referred to as *punishment* and *penalty*. As with all four consequences, when applied appropriately, they do work. Obviously, you would like to be able to stop behavior that you don't want. Unfortunately, consequences always affect behavior, so just as you can inadvertently reinforce behavior that you don't want, you also can inadvertently punish and extinguish behavior that you do want. If you and others in your organization are unaware of the effect of consequences on behavior, it is possible that you are stopping behavior that you want people to do. To understand more fully what is happening in your company, let's discuss the effects of punishment and penalty in detail.

Punishment and Penalty—Stopping Behavior

What do you do when people do things that are unsafe, unhealthy, unfair, unethical, or illegal? If possible, you act to stop these kinds of actions immediately because of the high level of potential damage they represent.

Punishment and penalty are active consequences that follow behavior and decrease its frequency in the future. As described in Chapter 4, punishment occurs when a behavior produces something the performer does not want. When a behavior results in the the loss of something that the performer values (time, money, freedom) that is called a penalty.

Although it is necessary to use punishment and penalty from time to time, they should be used sparingly. Both are difficult to use. Although they may decrease or stop behavior, they do not predict what behavior will replace the one you have stopped. Punishment and penalty should always be used in conjunction with positive reinforcement for the desired alternative behavior.

> Warning: Stopping problem behavior does not mean that a positive or productive behavior will take its place.

Much of the punishment that occurs in business is not planned—it's inadvertent. Everybody is familiar with the manager who "fusses at" the person who brings bad news, and can't understand why, after a while, no one will reveal problems.

Take the case of a fiberglass plant that was having a difficult time producing a particular product. The line had not met standard for almost two years and was running at a significant loss. The engineers had been unsuccessful in correcting the problem.

Finally, management decided to try a different approach. They got the employees from each shift together and asked for their input. On the first shift, when someone would make a suggestion, the engineer who was writing down the suggestions would ask follow-up questions to make sure that he knew exactly what the person was talking about.

On the second shift, everything was the same, but in this case the plant superintendent, an acknowledged expert in fiberglass manufacturing, was in attendance. Within the first 10 minutes, he jumped up three different times to show people why what they had suggested wouldn't work.

The first group produced over 50 suggestions. The second group produced only 6. The difference? In the second shift the superintendent punished people for their ideas. He didn't intend to; he just wanted to use this opportunity to teach the group something. Instead, every employee who offered an idea was made to feel stupid in front of his or her peers. The idea-giving behavior was stopped cold.

Different Strokes ...

Some of the same characteristics that make positive reinforcement effective also make punishment effective. Just as with positive reinforcement, what is punishing to one may not be punishing to others. Believe it or not, getting chewed out may be punishing to one person and positively reinforcing to another. The only way you can really tell is by what happens to the behavior after the chewing out.

In the same vein, delayed punishment is no more effective than delayed reinforcement. One of the things that reduces the effectiveness of the criminal justice system is the long delay between the commission of a crime and the start of the sentence. In organizations that have progressive discipline systems, the fact that someone progresses through the system tells you that the consequences are not punishing. But the amount of time that it takes to mete out the punishment is probably more important.

Look at your system to see what the average interval is from the infraction of the rules to the punishing consequence. Immediate consequences are the most effective, and any lengthy interval diminishes the effectiveness considerably. As with reinforcement, catching someone in the act is more effective than delayed action.

Punishment Never Solves a Problem

Because punishment only stops behavior, it does not add value to a business (or a family). The only reason we would want a person to stop an unproductive behavior is to replace it with a productive one. *Punishment doesn't tell people what you want them to do; it only tells them what not to do.* It is quite possible that you could stop one undesirable behavior and have another equally undesirable behavior take its place.

For this reason, you should never punish one behavior without knowing what you want in its place and reinforcing the desirable behavior soon as it occurs.

Recovery

One of the problems with the use of punishment and penalty to stop behaviors is that when they stop, if an alternate behavior is not reinforced, the old behavior will recover. Technically, *recovery* refers to the fact that punished behavior will return to nonpunished levels when the punishment or penalty is stopped.

The effect of getting a speeding ticket may last only until the trooper is out of sight. Why do most criminals go to jail many times over their lifetimes? Prison obviously did not stop the criminal activity permanently. When behaviors incompatible with criminal activity are not reinforced, you can expect that the old behavior will recover soon after the person finds himself or herself in an environment where there is no immediate threat of punishment or penalty. Punishment and penalty never solve a problem. At best, they stop behavior long enough for you to find a way to reinforce behavior that is productive.

Extinction—Doing Nothing Changes Behavior

There is another way behavior is stopped, and it is the most common way organizations unintentionally demotivate people. *Extinction* is what happens when a behavior occurs with no reinforcement. In other words, *extinction means withholding or not delivering reinforcement for previously reinforced behavior.*

Someone tells what she thinks is a funny joke. After the joke, the teller starts laughing hysterically. Then she suddenly realizes that no one else is laughing. Immediately, the joke teller stops laughing as well. If the same joke is told a couple more times with the same response, the individual will no doubt eliminate it from her repertoire.

In the same way, a new employee arrives on the scene believing that his best work is what is required, and he is more than willing to oblige. After a few months on the job "going the extra mile," the employee realizes that nobody notices. Like the joker in the preceding example, this person soon eliminates extra effort from his repertoire.

If you want a behavior or performance to continue, you must make sure that it is being reinforced. Because failing to reinforce previously reinforced productive performance is extinction, it's easy to see why performance and motivation drop off in even the best employees. The dropoff is an indication that employees are simply not getting the reinforcement they need to continue doing a good job. This is why the extinction of discretionary effort is almost assured in work environments where management is not making a conscious attempt to positively reinforce.

But there are behaviors that we want to eliminate, and at those times, the intentional use of extinction can be very helpful. We are all familiar with the saying, "Just ignore it, and it'll go away." This is basically how extinction works. However, as you might imagine, if it were that easy, we wouldn't have to deal with it in this book. To bring out the best in people, you need a much more complete understanding of extinction.

Let's look at an example to which everybody can relate. Mom and Dad are having trouble getting Johnny to sleep alone. When they put him to bed, he starts crying. His parents ignore him for a while, but after he cries for a few minutes, they go get him and bring him into their bed and he stops crying. They admonish him all the while that he must learn to sleep in his own bed, but he continues to sleep in theirs. A helpful relative suggests that it will not hurt the little boy if he is allowed to cry and assures the parents that if they leave him in his bed, he will stop crying after only a few nights.

What actually does happen is known to almost everybody. It goes like this:

1. The parents let the child cry for longer than usual.

2. He cries louder than usual.

3. The parents think something must be wrong.

4. They give in to him at this point, and he ends up in their bed and stops crying.

You probably know that the next night he will cry louder and longer. Let's assume that the parents don't go to him but rather they stick it out. If crying louder doesn't bring the parents, the child may begin to flail about in his crib, crying all the while. If the parents don't go in, he will eventually stop crying. After he is quiet for a few minutes, he may start crying again, but this time if his parents don't come in to get him, he will stop sooner than the night before.

This may go on for a few nights, but each night the crying will get shorter, and in a relatively short time, the behavior will stop—if the parents can stick with their plan for ignoring the crying. While this is not a business example, when you understand the different aspects of extinction in this problem, you will understand how to fix some of your motivational problems at work.

Extinction Burst

The first thing that happens when a well-developed behavior is ignored is an increase in that behavior. In other words, the behavior that is being extinguished actually will occur more often. We witness this in our everyday affairs. If we push the button for an elevator and it is slow to arrive, we then push the button several times in succession, although this has no effect on the elevator.

If we lose something, we probably look in the same places over and over. In an election, when a candidate begins to slip in the polls, she tries harder, makes more appearances, and criticizes the opponent more vehemently. If someone is a chronic complainer and you ignore the complaints, he actually may complain about more things, and with more agitation. This is a predictable and naturally occurring phenomenon. You can see it at every level of society.

At work, when you hear such things as, "We've got to get back to basics" or "We've got to try harder," you are hearing *extinction burst*. This means that behaviors that were productive have not received reinforcement and have undergone extinction. Doing the same things harder will rarely solve problems. If what was being done all along could have solved the problem, it would have already been solved. Doing the same thing harder is often an indication that the behavior is undergoing extinction.

Emotional Behavior

Following the extinction burst, you will usually see *negative emotional behavior*. The child flails about in his crib, the candidate gets more venomous, and the individual kicks the elevator door when it doesn't arrive in a timely way. If you are not prepared to handle the emotional behavior, you'd better not try to use extinction. It is not uncommon to see strikes settled during the emotional behavior phase, which, of course, increases the probability of violence in future strikes. Negative emotional behavior is further evidence that extinction is occurring.

Erratic Behavior

After the emotional behavior has run its course, the behavior will continue to occur at various irregular intervals until it stops altogether. Sometimes the behavior will be replaced by a similar behavior. It is during this period of erratic behavior that you must be careful not to reinforce new, undesired behavior. The amount of time it takes for the behavior to finally stop is affected by a number of variables, but in general the more reinforcement the person has received for the behavior in the past, the more time is required for extinction.

Resurgence

When the old behavior has stopped for a period of time, it is not unusual for it to occur again, seemingly out of nowhere. This has led many to believe that people don't really change. You see someone try to eliminate a habit, quit for a while, but eventually go back to the old ways.

The *resurgence* of the old habit is an indication that the behavior(s) that replaced it is(are) not getting enough reinforcement to stick. We see this in many people who try to quit smoking or drinking or who are trying to lose weight. They will have some initial success only to revert to the old habit.

The key to making extinction work to eliminate an unwanted behavior is to *introduce positive reinforcement for a productive alternative behavior.* For example, at work, there may be a person who constantly interrupts meetings with hostile, sarcastic comments. The group could put these comments on extinction by ignoring them. Then the group should positively reinforce constructive comments and questions.

When you want to extinguish behavior, you need to be prepared for the four previously mentioned aspects of extinction. If you don't think that you will be able to handle them all, you need to choose another consequence.

Problems in the workplace are often created not by what we do, but by what we fail to do.

Bringing out the best in people is not only about getting more of what you want but also about getting less of what you don't want. All four consequences I have presented have appropriate applications at work, but as with any skill, the use of behavioral consequences to manage people takes time to learn. There are right ways to use them, and there are attempts that fall short. I am going to present some very specific applications for all four consequences in the remainder of this book.

9

Effective Delivery of Reinforcement

If people are not told they are appreciated,
they will assume the opposite.

If positive reinforcement is so effective, why is it not used more commonly in business? One reason is that managers are more likely to be positively reinforced when they punish or use negative reinforcement than when they use positive reinforcement. Think back to the chapter on consequences (Chapter 4). You may recall that consequences that are positive, immediate, and certain (PIC) are much more powerful than those that are delayed (Future, as in PFU).

A manager is more likely to receive positive immediate consequences when delivering punishment than when delivering positive reinforcement. The reason? If punishment is going to work, it typically will work right away. The manager gets what she wants (usually some inappropriate behavior stops immediately), and this provides the manager with a PIC. The manager, like all of us, will tend to repeat that punishing behavior because it was reinforced. Likewise, negative reinforcement ("Do it or else!") will result in an increase in activity, providing the manager with positive reinforcement for the use of negative reinforcement.

When that same manager uses positive reinforcement, she will have to wait until there is an occasion for the behavior to occur again to know whether the reinforcement had any effect on the performer. In this case, the consequence for the manager is a positive, future, and uncertain consequence (PFU), not a powerful consequence.

Another reason that positive reinforcement is not the predominant consequence at work is that many managers have tried to use it and have been unsuccessful. I've heard many times, "Oh, I tried that reinforcement stuff, and it didn't work." Of course, by now you know that this can't happen. Reinforcement always works! It has to increase behavior or it isn't a reinforcer.

Common Mistakes in the Delivery of Positive Reinforcement

What I have discovered is that when managers complain that positive reinforcement doesn't work, they have made one of the following errors: perception, contingency, immediacy, or frequency. Let's consider each of these.

The Perception Error

As stated earlier, what works as a reinforcer for one person may not work for another. Many people will choose to use the reinforcers they like rather than finding what others like.

At times, we make the mistake of thinking people *should* want things that we want them to want. In other words, they should respond positively to the things we give them. There are many things managers think are reinforcing that are not. For example, most people assume that money is a reinforcer to everybody. Do you think that Donald Trump would find $100 reinforcing?

Many people do not find money reinforcing under certain circumstances. We have all said at one time or another, "You couldn't pay me enough to do that" or "I wouldn't work there for any amount of money."

Some managers think that if $1,000 is reinforcing to someone, then $100 would be *somewhat reinforcing* to that person. This is erroneous thinking. There are some things that you would be happy to do for $1,000 but wouldn't even lift a finger to do for $100. This mistake is also seen in the way we give raises and bonuses. The top performers get a 5 percent increase, and those at the level below them get 4 percent. Many outstanding performers have been heard to say in this situation, "If they think I'm going to break my back for a lousy 1 percent, they're crazy."

Similarly, have you ever heard someone say, "Everybody likes public recognition"? The fact is that in surveys I have done, most employees say that they don't like it. They give various reasons, but most of those reasons center on concern about what peers might think about them or know about them. They may worry that peers think they don't deserve the recognition. The effective manager or supervisor knows which people like public recognition and which people don't.

The most basic element in performance management is that you must first have a reinforcer. Make sure that you use some of the ways discussed in Chapter 7 to find an effective reinforcer. Once you have a reinforcer, you are on your way, but there are still some things that could cause it to be ineffective.

The Contingency Error

This error relates to the relationship between a behavior and a reinforcer. If you can get a reinforcer without engaging in a prerequisite behavior, then that reinforcer is said to be *noncontingent*. If the *only* way you can get a reinforcer is to engage in a particular behavior, that reinforcer is said to be *contingent on that behavior*. For example, in the average company, an increase in fringe benefits may not increase performance because fringe benefits are provided to everyone regardless of performance. Improved fringe benefits are given whether or not a given employee's performance increases. The fringe benefits are said to be noncontingent.

To say that hard work pays off implies that there is a reinforcement contingency between hard work and pay and/or promotions. Many people will tell you that if there is a contingency between work and pay, it is a loose one because they work hard and don't get increases in pay.

Profit sharing is often administered noncontingently. One reason it loses its effectiveness is that there is only an indirect contingency between profit and the performance of any given individual. In many companies, if there is profit, it is shared on the basis of some predetermined formula, which is independent of a given person's performance. Therefore, if there is a profit, everyone will share just because they are on the payroll.

Salespeople sometimes "earn" commissions not because of what they did but because they were lucky enough to have a customer who uses the company's product. If they were not using sound sales behaviors to cause the sale to close, the commission may inadvertently reinforce behaviors that represent poor sales techniques and will lead to poor performance in the future.

Make a list of reinforcers and rewards in your organization, and state the behavioral contingency in the following format:

You can get … if and only if you …

To use a previous example, "You can get a *bonus* if and only if *you are on the payroll.*" If you make such a list, you will be surprised at how few reinforcers are contingent on productive, quality, and safe behaviors. You will be enlightened and reinforced at the same time because you will immediately see solutions to some of your problems.

The Delay Error

I explained the importance of immediate reinforcement earlier. If someone said to me, "I don't have time to reinforce," my response would be, "In that case, you'd better reinforce immediately." The longer you wait after the behavior, the less effective the reinforcement will be. The error is delaying the positive reinforcement. If you have a limited amount of time to spend in the activity of reinforcing, spend it reinforcing desirable behavior while the behavior is occurring.

Most leadership research is based on what leaders *say* they do. Dr. Judi Komaki (1986) is one of very few people who have done research on what leaders *actually do*. What Dr. Komaki has found is that the most effective leaders, managers, and supervisors do not necessarily reinforce more often than the ineffective ones. What they do is *reinforce while people are performing*. To be able to do this, they spend more time in the work area observing behavior. Where do you think the ineffective supervisors spend their time? You guessed it—in their offices.

The only behavior a supervisor can reinforce in his office would be whatever the person is doing in the supervisor's office. Ironically, most supervisory duties today take the supervisor out of the workplace and into an office or a meeting room.

When reinforcement is immediate, you know what you are reinforcing because it is happening before your eyes. The longer reinforcement is delayed, the less sure you are of which behavior is actually being reinforced because people are continuously behaving.

The greatest advantage of teams (and one that is almost always overlooked) is that team members can provide immediate reinforcement to each other. If team members are taught to deliver positive reinforcement, they are in the best position to make it immediate. In most cases, they are also in the best position to know whose behavior merits reinforcement.

The Frequency Error

One positive reinforcer will not change your life. "I reinforced him, but he didn't change" is an oft-stated complaint. It is not that managers don't understand the need for reinforcement and recognition; it is that they don't have an understanding of the amount of reinforcement that is needed to create peak performers and a high-performance organization.

A case can be made for the fact that a little reinforcement is better than none at all, but in the amounts given in many organizations, it is not much better. To give you a perspective on frequency, in *The Technology of Teaching*, B. F. Skinner states that it may take as many as 50,000 reinforcers to teach competence in basic math—roughly the first four grades.

This works out to more than 70 reinforcers per hour per student. Although getting the correct answer in math is a reinforcer, the delay between doing a math problem in a traditional classroom and knowing whether it is correct could be several days. Computer-aided instruction helps because the computer lets the student know immediately if the answer is correct, but the number of problems to be solved per class is not enough for students to gain fluency in the math operation tested. Also, the number of *attempts* at verbal reinforcement varies widely from teacher to teacher, but the median number found in several studies is about six per hour. When you understand this relationship of reinforcement to learning, you can understand the problems we are experiencing in the schools today.

Students simply do not get enough reinforcement to maximize learning. I would not want to suggest that the number of reinforcers that adults need to acquire a new skill or make substantial improvement in an existing way of doing something is equal to what a child needs in school. However, it certainly gives you a perspective on what it takes to make significant changes in behavior. With this frame of reference, everybody should understand that an occasional reinforcer at work will make only a small difference in performance.

The way that many organizations think about frequency may be seen in *annual* performance appraisals, *annual* recognition dinners, *quarterly* bonuses, employees of the *month*, and so on. This low frequency of reinforcement will have little or no impact on organizational performance. Positive reinforcement needs to be a daily affair.

The 4:1 Rule

Years ago, when I first started working in industry, I was often asked, "What is the proper balance between positive reinforcement and punishment?" This question was sometimes phrased as, "How many 'atta-boys' does it take to erase one 'You really screwed that up!'" In researching the literature, I found two studies that I think have some bearing on the question.

Madsen (1974), in training classroom teachers, found that teachers who had positive reinforcement-to-punishment ratios of 4:1 or better had good discipline and high achievement in their classrooms. Below these ratios, they had problems. Stuart (1971), in a study of delinquent children, found similar ratios with parents of nondelinquent and delinquent children. Parents with no delinquent children had higher ratios of positive interactions than parents of delinquents. Hart and Risley (1995) found that vocabulary development in young children was dramatically accelerated in families in which the ratio of positive to negative interactions was high (approximately 6:1).

White (1975) and Thomas (1968) studied naturally occurring ratios in classrooms and found ratios in the range of 1:2. Self-reports by supervisors and managers revealed ratios of 2:1 at best. The ratios reported are probably more positive than the naturally occurring rates because the rates were taken as a part of a class in performance management. Few would disagree that there is a lot of room for improving the ratio of positive reinforcement to punishment in most organizations.

Some people have misunderstood the 4:1 rule. It does not mean that if you reinforce four times, you have to punish something. The ratio can be higher than 4:1. In a high-performing organization, punishment may be infrequent indeed, but it is unrealistic to expect that there will be no occasion for negative consequences in any organization over a period of time. If you have a work environment where there are never any negatives, it probably means that you are positively reinforcing some poor performance.

Check your own ratios. Keep a three-by-five-inch card, and tally all your attempts at reinforcement and punishment each day. If the ratio is less than 4:1, work on increasing your attempts at positive reinforcement. The card will be an antecedent for looking for opportunities to reinforce. Remember to reinforce only behavior or performance that warrants it. Many improvements have been reported in quality and productivity when supervisors simply increased their daily frequency of contingent positive reinforcement.

Competition for Positive Reinforcement

When there is too little reinforcement to go around, people will compete with each other to get it. Competition for significant reinforcers and rewards, financial or social, can generate behavior that is incompatible with the team-oriented work environment that most organizations are trying to promote. Infrequent reinforcement promotes the kind of "political" behaviors with which we are all familiar: blaming others, covering your rear, and even sabotaging the initiatives of others.

People should not be exerting effort to compete for reinforcement within your company. If you want employees to compete, you should focus them on external competitors. Because we have all grown up in a competitive society, we assume that internal competition is an acceptable model for business. I suggest that internal competition isn't a good model. A company should focus employees on performing better than their competition and not on their teammates.

In obviously competitive circumstances (such as sports), competition within the team becomes visibly counterproductive very quickly. When a basketball player takes a shot when he should have passed the ball to a teammate, everybody on the team and in the stands knows it. In football, when a teammate steps in front of the intended receiver to catch a pass, everyone clearly sees it. At work, it is not as easy to see behaviors that cause others to fail or to have a more difficult job.

We certainly want our employees to be competitive. But we want them competing within our industry, not within our company. We don't want people to fight for reinforcement. We want reinforcement to be available for all who earn it.

Employee of the Month

When you think about the principles described in this chapter, it becomes obvious that *employee of the month* (EOM) and other such recognition programs violate every rule of effective positive reinforcement. I will describe later how to fix EOM and other recognition and reward programs, but for now, let me just say that EOM not only doesn't reinforce the behaviors you want, but it may in fact be punishing them.

If you have such a program in your organization, think about the following: Does the award go to the best performer every month? Does the performance of the recipient improve after he or she receives the award? Can you identify the specific behaviors that the award is reinforcing? Do you know if the actual award is something that the recipient likes? If you answered no to any of these questions, cancel the EOM program now. If you answered, "I don't know," take a closer look and be prepared to alter your approach,

Two Attempts at Positive Reinforcers That Aren't

The "No But" Rule.   When supervisors and managers are asked, "Do you tell people that they are doing a good job?," they practically always say that they do. When you ask employees, "Do your supervisors tell you that you do a good job?," they practically always respond, "They don't."

My analysis of this is that managers actually say the words, "You did a good job" or "I appreciate what you did." However, they don't stop there. Frequently, they go on to say something like *"but you could have done … ."* As is often taught in sales training, "Don't talk yourself out of a sale!"

A complete example may sound something like this: *"You did a good job compiling the final project report, but it would have been even better if you had included the original documents as an appendix."* From the perspective of the supervisor making this statement, he has taken the time to reinforce the behavior of "compiling the final project report" and has mentioned a little helpful hint: "Next time include the original documents as an appendix." Although well intended, this statement probably would be more punishing than reinforcing.

John Domenick, a performance management consultant, said it well: "Good intentions are terrible things to waste." When the supervisor added the word "but," he turned a positive statement into a negative with a single word. You see, *"but" is a verbal eraser* when used in an attempt to praise. It erases everything that preceded it. The reinforcement is gone. The criticism remains.

The president of a nationally known dairy products company once told me that he received a call from the chairman of the board of his company's holding company. The call started off, "John, I was just looking at your financial results from last year. You set a record. It was the best the company has ever done." At this point, the president said that he was feeling great. However, the chairman went on to say, "but if you had had a better handle on your inventory during the second quarter, you could have done even better." John said that he was devastated immediately and got angry later. I'm quite sure the chairman is certain he complimented John for a good job. If asked, he would probably say that John knows how much he appreciates his work. I know that John did not feel either complimented or appreciated. *Do not use the occasion for praise as an opportunity to prompt or instruct.*

The Sandwich.   The so-called sandwich method of correcting performance is probably the most widely taught concept in basic supervisory training. A variation of the "no but" rule, the sandwich is a negative between two positives. It goes like this:

Positive: "Thad, you are one of the best employees I've got."

Negative: "But if your attendance doesn't improve, I'm going to have to terminate you."

Positive: "You know, you have more talent in your little finger than most people have in their whole body. I would hate to lose you."

Some psychologists say that this method preserves one's self-esteem in the process of correcting. I know of no experimental data that demonstrate this fact. I think that it helps the punisher by making the feedback easier. At best, it is confusing to the performer. After all, there were two positive comments and only one negative. In addition, when do you think Thad will hear positive statements like this again? Probably not until he is in trouble again.

Sandwiching is not a good practice. Criticism should be short and to the point. You should be very clear regarding which behavior must increase or stop, what will happen if it does, and what to do instead. Positives should be saved until there is some improvement in performance.

Do not pair positive reinforcement with punishment.

Our example would have been better handled like this: "Thad your attendance has put your employment in jeopardy. If you miss one more day during the rest of this quarter, you will be terminated. I hope this will not be necessary. If there is anything I can do to help you, let me know." Later that day, when he is doing his job, you could approach Thad and say something like, "Thad, I hated to have to get on you this morning. You're one of the best employees I've got."

While this may appear to be a trivial difference, I assure you it will produce a very different result. Because showing concern is usually positive to most people, the pairing of concern with good work probably will act as a positive reinforcer for the productive performance. If concern is paired only with problem performance, you will likely get more problem performance.

A Case of Positive Imprecision

A plant manager once asked me if I would talk to one of his department supervisors to see if he was "cut out to be in management." The plant manager thought that because I was a psychologist, I would be able to analyze the supervisor's management potential. As a matter of fact, the management staff had already decided to terminate this supervisor because the general foreman didn't think he was management material.

I explained that it would be difficult to make a recommendation just by talking with the supervisor. I suggested that if the manager was serious about making an informed decision, he should put the supervisor through the scheduled performance management training and see how he responded. I would then have some data about his effectiveness and could help the plant manager make a better judgment.

As was discovered in class, the young supervisor was *too* positive. That is, he attempted to reinforce everyone, violating the contingency principle many times a day. When his reinforcement attempts didn't work, he started using the negative management style of most of his peers. Since he didn't like managing that way, his heart was not in it, and he had become totally ineffective.

When he learned about contingency, immediacy, and frequency, the performance of his shift changed dramatically, almost overnight. I don't know the end of this story because it hasn't been written yet, but the last I heard was that the young supervisor was then a plant manager.

Most managers using atta-boys, pats on the back, and other positive management techniques typically commit some or all of the reinforcement errors mentioned in this chapter. They are usually well-meaning individuals who are not aware of the precision required in the effective delivery of positive reinforcement. Because of this, they are usually ineffective in bringing out the best in people.

However, these managers are usually predisposed toward being positive. When they learn to avoid these errors, they are able to increase their personal effectiveness dramatically and in a short period of time.

Some supervisors claim that they follow all the rules discussed in this chapter, and it still doesn't work. This brings up the *relationship issue*. If the person on the receiving end of your reinforcing attempts doesn't like or respect you, telling the employee that you appreciate her work will not work. If the employee knows that you say one thing to her face and another, or the opposite, thing behind her back, then telling her that she is doing a good job may have the opposite effect on her performance and, if I may use the term, her attitude.

My mother once told me that my brother, a high school teacher, had received a nice letter from the assistant county superintendent about his work. Later I asked him why he had not told me about it. He said, "It didn't mean anything. He sent that same letter to all the teachers in the county."

For all new supervisors or managers, the first task is to pair your presence with positive reinforcers. I was an artillery officer stationed in Korea, and we had a high turnover of officers because rotation back home was looked toward from the first day. Unfortunately, many of the officers, from their first day, wanted to show everyone that they knew more than the troops did. These officers had a very difficult time. However, a few of them spent the first few days getting to know each soldier personally, asking about their families and where they grew up and went to school and asking about their job in the battery. In almost every case, they did not act like a know-it-all but like a student, having the soldier teach them something. As you can imagine, the first ones spent much time in the battery commander's office explaining some problem or other, whereas the latter always had troops "at their back."

When you do positive reinforcement correctly, it makes hard work fun while accomplishing much. Done wrong, it makes easy tasks difficult and accomplishes little.

PART 3

The Scientific Approach to Leadership

10
Pinpointing

If you don't know where you are going,
any road will take you there.

—A<small>NONYMOUS</small>

If It's Working, Find Out Why

The president of a manufacturing company, aware of my experience as a clinical psychologist, asked me to explain why a really top performer (plant manager) would "become almost useless overnight." "Could it be drugs, alcohol, stress, family problems, or something like that?" he asked. I said it was possible, but I needed to know more.

He then described a performance problem in a plant in Louisiana and continued, "We decided the plant manager had failed to take any action, so we let him go and promoted the assistant plant manager to take his place. The new plant manger did a great job, and things turned around almost immediately. Not too long after that, we began having trouble with a larger plant in Virginia, so we moved him there. Shortly after his arrival, the plant was doing much better. Now we've brought him to our home base, where we have our largest plant, and his performance is a disaster. I can't believe how unorganized he is. He doesn't plan well; he doesn't follow through; he changes priorities from day to day. He seems confused. What would cause such a change?"

"What did he do to turn the plant around in Louisiana?" I asked.

"I don't know," he replied.

"What did he do to turn the plant around in Virginia?"

"I don't know," he repeated.

"Then what makes you think he is doing anything different now?"

"I don't know," he said.

I don't think the plant manager was doing anything different in his third assignment than he had done in the first two plants. Circumstances, rather than his behavior, probably accounted for the difference in results.

This company was managed solely by results. As long as the results were there, little attention was paid to how the results were attained. In many organizations in this country, if you are getting results, management leaves you alone, and managers spend their time with those who are not getting results. This is an ineffective and very risky management practice.

As a lieutenant in the Army, I heard many times, "I don't care how you get it—just get it!" In the 1950s and 1960s, organizations using this same strategy seemed unconcerned with how results were achieved. Business was booming and getting results at almost any personnel or production cost. The increased costs were simply passed on to the consumer. Today, with even tougher competition and significantly heightened social awareness, organizations must be vigilant about *how* results are attained or face serious economic, social, and legal consequences.

Today, it is not enough to know that something is working. We need to know why it works. This point is very clear. If you don't know why something works, how will you know how to fix it when things go wrong or circumstances change?

You cannot truly manage by results alone. Getting results is critical to an organization's survival and success. No organization can survive without them. However, short-term results can be achieved by using totally inappropriate behavior. The sales representative who cuts a deal that is impossible for the company to honor and the manager who fudges on the numbers to make production figures look good are just a couple of examples in which the ends are not justified by the means. Short-term results can be achieved in ways that will drive up costs and damage quality and safety later. We must always be interested in and very knowledgeable about how results are attained.

Unfortunately, we sometimes pay attention to behaviors only when the results turn sour. The cause of the *Exxon Valdez* oil spill was inappropriate behavior that had been tolerated or ignored for some time. The crew and the captain engaged in behaviors other than those that would safely guide the oil tanker through the waters. The press reported that the captain had an alcohol problem, but his past results were sufficient, and Exxon officials had ignored the behaviors related to this problem until it was too late.

Other disastrous examples of results-only management include the savings and loan and insider-trading scandals that signaled the end of the winner-takes-all mentality of the 1980s. In every one of these cases, inappropriate behaviors produced positive short-term results—and long-lasting negative ones. This kind of management might more appropriately be called "management by autopsy" because it is only after some problem that an investigation is launched. From a behavioral perspective, because there are no behaviors to be seen at the time of the investigation, it can only be assumed that behavioral causes and assumptions are erroneous.

Sustaining results requires precise management. Managers need to know precisely which outcomes are required *and precisely what behaviors produce them*. The procedure for specifying results *and* behaviors is *pinpointing*. Pinpointing means being specific about a result you want and then being very specific about the behaviors required to achieve that result.

Beware of the Activity Trap: Pinpoint Results First

At the annual governor's conference in August 1993, President Clinton commented that when he was governor of Arkansas, he was excited about going to work every day because he knew that he would be able to accomplish some things that day. He observed that when he went to Washington, people seemed to be more concerned with the process of getting something done than they were with the product. He commented, "It's the darndest [*sic*] thing I've ever seen."

Although the element most often missing in the pinpointing process is the behavior pinpoint, it is still very important to pinpoint results first. You need both, but you should *always pinpoint results before you pinpoint behaviors*. While this sounds obvious, it's commonplace today for organizations to start programs that require people to change the way they work, with only a general idea of the results they want to achieve.

This is particularly true in the human relations area, where certain behaviors are assumed to have value. Teams, participative management, and employee engagement initiatives, for example, are often "sacred cows," whose real value to the organization is seldom questioned. Frequently, these programs are initiated without any direct ties to specific results. Many organizations have found themselves spending a lot of time and money with little or no return.

For example, the 1992 Initial Quality Study showed that cross-functional teams that include the customer did not always result in improved performance. An unpublished study conducted at Auburn University in 1991 by Dr. Bill Hopkins also found no evidence that self-directed teams are an effective means of achieving important organizational objectives. Hopkins further reported that "[w]e have not found one published paper that reports clear increases in areas such as productivity, quality of production, or sales or clear declines in areas such as absenteeism, scrap, or maintenance costs."

General statements such as "improved morale," "better decisions," and "personal pride" make great slogans, but they don't represent tangible pinpointed results. Programs are rarely measured and evaluated against such nonspecific outcomes.

Pinpoint the specific results you want first. Then identify the behaviors necessary to produce those results. If you know precisely which result you want, you can then test the relationship between the behaviors you think will get it and the actual accomplishment. You should never assume that you already know the behaviors that will produce the results. *Always evaluate changes in behavior against changes in results.*

One of our clients, an electrical connector manufacturer, made the error of thinking it knew the critical selling behaviors for its product. Sales management directed the sales force to call on architects to persuade them to specify the company's product in their architectural designs. Sales management assumed that this behavior was the best way to sell more of the company's product. But it was difficult to get appointments with the architects, and the sales managers had to constantly prod their salespeople to keep after the architects and chide salespeople for not obtaining appointments with the architects more often.

As a part of our work on improving the effectiveness of the company's sales management, we audited the sales reps' performance. One of the things we did was follow the best salespeople to observe what they did to make sales. The audit results shocked management because the data showed that their best salespeople spent almost no time with architects. They spent most of their time with distributors.

The behavior that produced the best sales results was calling on the distributors and convincing them to use the company's product regardless of what had been specified by the architect. The assumption of which behaviors would result in sales was based on someone's intuition rather than on actual observation and solid evidence.

Pinpoints Are Not Inside the Person

To use pinpointing effectively, it is necessary to remember one very important rule: pinpoints are real. They are tangible, observable results and behaviors, not beliefs, attitudes, or anything else internal, subjective, or abstract, but something you can see. Terms such as *motivation, personality, communication*, and *rapport* are useful when we are communicating informally, but when we need to change performance, they are not useful because they create prejudice and build obstacles to progress. Correcting or improving some performance or outcome requires precise pinpointing.

Labels such as "lazy," "lacks drive," and "bad attitude" imply that the problem—and therefore the solution to the problem—is within the person. Using labels to describe performance not only can't help change the performance, but it also produces blame. We blame the performer for being unmotivated, having a bad attitude, needing too much attention, or not having enough drive. When you approach a problem this way, the only solution is to tell the person to "shape up or ship out."

Another problem with these performer stereotypes is that even if, as a manager, you accept the responsibility to "change someone," if you don't have a pinpointed behavior, you don't know which behavior to change. The reason most people think that you can't change a person's attitude or personality is that what is generally referred to as *personality* is actually a collection of many behaviors. To change someone's attitude requires that you pinpoint the behaviors that make up the attitude. If you can pinpoint the behaviors, you can, at least, change them one at a time. If over time you change some or all of the behaviors, you certainly will change an individual's personality. The process of pinpointing gives you a realistic place to start the change process.

In the Eye of the Beholder. What do we mean when we say a person has a positive attitude? We could be referring to the fact that the individual is always on time, or seldom complains, or keeps the work area exceptionally clean, or volunteers to help others, or smiles and jokes, or maintains high productivity and quality. In other words, we could characterize a person as having a positive attitude if he did any one or a few of those things or all of them.

The same is also true for performers with a bad attitude. They, too, demonstrate a pattern of behaviors that results in a negative label. Once you realize that a bad attitude is composed of many behaviors, it's easy to understand why *attitude* is so difficult to change or remedy. Flushing out and pinpointing the specific and observable behaviors that make up the bad attitude or cause you to label the person as negative or uncooperative are essential if you are to effectively change the performer's attitude.

Labels Don't Provide Answers.   Using vague phrases or labels to describe problem performance does nothing to change or improve performance. Calling someone lazy or worthless fails to provide the necessary information needed to change behavior. The productive question to ask is, "Which specific behaviors cause me to label this person lazy?" Turning in projects late? Turning in messy work? Failing to follow through with customers and coworkers on important assignments? These are specific questions that can lead to specific answers.

What to Do . . .   For some managers, pinpointing is the most difficult and time-consuming part of managing performance. We always seem to know more about what we don't want people to do than what we want them to do. We issue directives such as, Don't make errors, Don't have accidents, and Don't be late. What we must keep in mind is that people are hired to do things. Active behavior gets things done.

If, for example, someone is making mistakes in data entry on an assembly procedure, telling the person to stop making errors will not solve your problem because *one way of not making errors is to do nothing*. Errors are always a measure of something other than the behavior of interest, so you will not necessarily get what you want by stopping what you don't want. If you tell people to stop using their cell phones while working, for example, they may stop the calls but talk to coworkers instead. Pinpointing behavior requires finding what people need to do, not what they don't do.

The importance of pinpointing *active behaviors* was made clear by Dr. Ogden Lindsley. In 1965 he developed the *dead-man's test*, which is "If a dead man can do it, it isn't behavior, and you shouldn't waste your time trying to produce it."

Yet much of what we typically track in quality and safety violates the dead-man's test. "Zero defects" and "days without a lost-time accident" are prime examples of popular goals that violate the dead-man's test. Dead men never have accidents, and they never produce defective parts.

If you examine a typical business, you'll see numerous examples of management focusing on inactive behavior or behavior that leads to no accomplishment. Some people think that this active versus inactive dimension of pinpointing is really two sides of the same coin—that it's more a problem of semantics than a real problem. Not so.

One day I looked out the window of my office and saw two young carpenters just as they finished paneling the roof of a new building in our office park before putting on the shingles.

As crazy as it may sound, one of them proceeded to do a handstand on the crown of the roof. He then walked on his hands from one end of the building to the other, a distance of about 60 feet. Not to be outdone, his coworker followed close behind. Obviously, this was something the two athletic young men had done many times before. It was certainly not safe behavior, but neither fell, and they ended the job with "no lost-time accidents." Using the criteria of the usual safety program, these two could easily qualify as participants at their employer's safety celebration commemorating a million hours without a lost-time accident. As you can see, no "lost-time accidents" doesn't necessarily reflect the level of safe behaviors on the job; it just reflects a fortunate result. In the same way, zero defects do not equal careful quality-oriented behavior. Even though the day of the explosion on the Horizon deep-water oil platform in 2010 there was a celebration of seven years of operation without a lost-time accident, the safety report showed many failures to perform correct monitoring and repair of items that posed potential risks. It is quite possible that many unsafe behaviors occurred every day of the seven years without a lost-time accident. Monitoring results without observing the behaviors that produce them may cause disastrous results.

If It Doesn't Move, It's a Result

Like behaviors, results also can be more precisely pinpointed. Gilbert (1978) developed a test for determining whether you have an accomplishment. He called his test the *leave-it test*. The leave-it test works this way: if you can leave it behind when you walk out of the office or plant, it is a result. If it's something you take with you, it is not. For example, "safety awareness" cannot be left behind at the end of the day and therefore would not meet Gilbert's definition of a result.

Safety awareness, better communication, and increased teamwork are not pinpointed results, and effort spent trying to produce them may consume considerable financial and personnel resources, generating little value to the organization. These phrases are descriptions of a problem and, as such, represent only a beginning to solving it. You must pinpoint the desired result more precisely if you are to solve problems reliably and efficiently.

Behaviors and results define performance, and you need both to run an efficient and effective organization. So how do you pinpoint?

Precision Pinpointing

Pinpointing means being specific about results and behaviors. It requires *precise descriptions* of results and behaviors that are can be reliably *observed and measured*.

Observability

Seeing is believing. In the final analysis, business has to be interested in results and behaviors that can be seen. Pinpointing observable results is relatively easy. This is why we have focused on them for so long. The problem of observability comes up when we try to pinpoint behavior. Factors that affect behavior but are not observable, such as thoughts and emotions, are not the province of management. We can't expect line managers, or anyone for that matter, to delve into the inner feelings of others. The good news is we don't have to. You can manage yourself and others very successfully by limiting yourself to pinpointing behaviors that you can see and hear.

Measurability

Many people, when faced with these characteristics of good pinpoints, immediately complain that these criteria (especially measurement) will limit the pinpoints they can identify. This is not the case. *The fact is that if something is happening, it can be measured.* Every behavior can be measured in terms of frequency or duration or both. Even when something is not happening, it is being measured. The measure is zero. Some things may not be worth measuring, but if it is important, it can be measured. (Measurement will be explained in detail in Chapter 11.)

Reliability

The third characteristic of a valid pinpoint is reliability. When two or more people can observe a behavior or result and come up with the same count or measure, you have a true pinpoint.

Have you ever heard someone described as "friendly" by one coworker and then described as "aloof" by someone else? They are either observing or measuring different things or their measures are not reliable. This example from the *American Journalism Review* will show you what I mean:

> From the *Washington Post*, January 15:
>
>> "Donna E. Shalala . . . at her confirmation hearing . . . faced little in the way of tough questioning. . . ."
>
> From the *New York Times*, same day:
>
>> ". . . Shalala encountered tough questioning today. . . ."
>
> From the *Washington Post*, January 16:
>
>> "Diary Says Bush Knew 'Details' of Iran Arms Deal"
>
> From the *New York Times*, same day:
>
>> "Entries Suggest [Bush] Did Not Know Details . . ."

Refining observations to the point of reliability is an important skill in pinpointing. We may often start with a pinpoint that is not totally reliable, but as we use it, measure it, and discuss our observations, we can refine it until it becomes more and more reliable. Even journalists could be trained to do this.

Counts of Behaviors Versus Results

As I pointed out at the beginning of this chapter, behavior is what a person does, and a result is what is produced by the behaviors. Differentiating the two is sometimes difficult when you first begin pinpointing.

A count of behavior is sometimes confused with important organizational results. Behavior counts (e.g., number of times one of your staff gets reports in on time, number of times one of your peers disrupts a staff meeting with jokes, or number of days an employee arrives on time) are important measures of behavior if your goal is to reduce or increase that behavior, but they are not results.

Some organizations require employees to attend a fixed number of hours of training each year. Is this a valuable result or a count of behaviors? I consider attendance at training as merely a count of behaviors. The valuable result should be measured in terms of on-the-job performance.

Results are usually defined as some outcome that is valuable to the organization: number of defect-free items produced, increased revenue per sale, or reduction of cycle time. Of course, it is important to measure both behaviors and results, but you should avoid confusing the two.

Figure 10-1, from *Performance Management: Improving Quality Productivity Through Positive Reinforcement*, will help you to differentiate behaviors from results.

Control of the Pinpoint

One of the important considerations in pinpointing a behavior or result you would like to change is to make sure that the behaviors and/or results are under the performer's control. Care must be given to identifying pinpoints that are within the influence of the performer.

Behavior	Results
1. What people are doing.	1. What people have produced.
2. What you see people do when they are working.	2. What you see after people stop working.
3. Must see people working.	3. Not necessary to see people working.
4. Tends to be expressed in present tense, verbs ending in ing.	4. Tends to be expressed in the past tense by noun-adjective pairings: documents filed.
5. Cue words: by, through, to.	5. Cue words and phrases: in order to, so that, to achieve, to be able to.
6. Commonly used terms: input, process, activity, means.	6. Commonly used terms: output, product, outcome, achievement, ends.
7. Examples: inspecting, designing, conducting meetings, reinforcing, giving feedback.	7. Examples: Production, yield, run time, milestones met, suggestions made.

Figure 10-1   Points for distinguishing behaviors from results.

Two examples come to mind. On the production floor, frontline employees do not typically control cost. Someone in purchasing does that. Employees control use of materials and supplies that have an impact on cost.

Frontline employees don't usually control units produced per day either. Production control may cut the production schedule or increase it. In these situations, the performer controls only the number of units produced per hour when material is available.

When developing pinpoints, it's important to specify the results performers control. *A rule of thumb is to describe the results that are as close as possible to the behaviors that produce them.*

Although few people in business today have total control over results, the control requirement is usually satisfied if a person or group has more control over the pinpoint than anyone else. One test for control is to ask, "If the performer did nothing, would the result change dramatically?"

Another way to determine whether a performer has control over results is to look at the data. If there are wild swings in the data from day to day, the performer probably doesn't have control. Also, if the data never vary, the performer probably doesn't have control either. If there are minor variations from shift to shift or performer to performer, then the performer likely is in control of much of the result. The only way you can know whether the performer is really in control is to correlate change in behavior with change in results.

In summary, when you can pinpoint results and behaviors that are active, measurable, observable, reliable, and under the control of the performers, you will have taken the first step toward being able to bring out the best in people.

11

The Effective Use of Measurement

When I worked as a clinical psychologist, I never had a patient complain about being measured. The reason: they never doubted that measurement was being used to help them with their problems. In business, measurement is also used to solve problems, to help a company perform better, not necessarily its employees. One of the most frequent uses of measurement is to identify performers who aren't measuring up (no pun intended). Based on the measurement, negative action is usually taken to correct the performance problem. No wonder employees avoid measurement whenever they can. It's no fun being identified as the problem or having measures paired with poor or substandard performance.

The purpose of measurement in a performance management system is different. Rather than using measurement to find problem employees, *measurement is used to enable employees to do better*, which, of course, should help the company perform better. When you understand the difference between the way measurement is used traditionally and the way it should be used, you will understand how to create conditions under which employees seek measurement rather than avoid it.

Myth: What Gets Measured Gets Done

In my performance management seminars, the item on the agenda that attracts the most interest is measurement. A great many people in business think that measuring a problem is tantamount to solving it. But as important as measurement is, measurement alone will not create lasting behavior change.

If measurement changed behavior, there would be no fat people, no one would smoke, and everyone would exercise because all these behaviors and their results can be easily measured. Many people know exactly how much they weigh and want to weigh less and know how many cigarettes they smoke and want to smoke less. But measuring doesn't change a thing. So what does measurement do for us?

In most cases, measurement is an antecedent. Unfortunately, in business, it is most often an antecedent to punishment or negative reinforcement. About every year or so the *Wall Street Journal* carries a story about a company having problems as a result of a new measurement system. Employees complain that they don't even have time to go to the bathroom or that they are being watched every moment. The following is an excerpt from a *New York Times* article on Amazon:

> Warehouses, employees are monitored by sophisticated electronic systems to ensure they are packing enough boxes every hour. (Amazon came under fire in 2011 when workers in an eastern Pennsylvania warehouse toiled in more than 100-degree heat with ambulances waiting outside, taking away laborers as they fell.)[1]

Why would you run a company like this? Because, as I previously explained, these new measurement systems seem to get improvements almost immediately.

By now you should know how such systems typically get the improvements—with *negative reinforcement*. If the company establishes a range of acceptable performance, and if that range is higher than previous expectations, the company will see improvement because the employees quickly realize that by maintaining their performance within that range, they can avoid punishment. You know that measurement is a negative reinforcer when you hear comments like, "You can't measure what I do." This is not an attempt to avoid measurement; it's an attempt to avoid punishment.

The ability to measure is not now nor has it ever been the problem. We can measure any performance. The problem comes from the way measurement is used. If it is used to punish, people will go to extraordinary lengths to avoid being measured. Falsification of data is a more common problem than many upper managers realize, and its main purpose is to avoid punishment.

When It's Done Right

Believe it or not, you can create an environment where people will want to be measured. I have seen it time and time again. When measurement is used to increase positive reinforcement, people will look forward to being measured. In these cases, if management doesn't provide measurement, people will devise it for themselves. A trucking company I worked with developed a positive measurement environment. When I visited there several years ago, a mechanic showed me a graph and with obvious pride pointed out that his group had found ways to reduce (by more than half) the number of hours it took to rebuild an engine. In addition, the quality was so good the group guaranteed the rebuilt engines for more miles than the original equipment.

In the company's tire recapping department, the recappers showed me a similar result. When old tires came in, the first thing employees did was check the serial number and truck odometer to see how many miles the recapped tires had run.

A supervisor in the accounting department showed me a note from a part-time employee. It read, "Mr. Smith, can I please have a graph like Mary Jo's? P.S.: I did 32 invoices in 45 minutes. I timed myself."

Obviously, measurement held no fear for these employees.

In another case, I sat in on a performance management review at AG Communications Company and heard a senior engineer report on his progress. He displayed a graph that indicated that he had more than doubled his productivity on software development. He commented to the group: "I'm pleased with the increase in productivity, but it has caused me to worry that I may be sacrificing quality. I don't think I am, but to make sure, I have figured out a way to measure my quality and will start using that measurement on Monday."

Overcoming Resistance to Measurement

If the people in your organization try to avoid or delay attempts to install job measurement and you want to begin measuring more precisely, there are two things you should do:

1. Increase the frequency of positive reinforcement for desirable behaviors as they are now occurring in the workplace.

2. Pair reinforcement with existing measures.

The length of time you must do these two things before introducing the new measures will vary depending on your history of using measurement to punish and your ability to increase effective positive reinforcement. However, if you use these two techniques for a couple of months, in most cases you will have a much easier time installing a new measurement system.

How to Measure

There are two basic ways to measure: counting and judging. *Counting* is generally recognized as the best way to measure because it is more objective. Frequency counts generally yield the best data.

Judging is generally more subjective and takes a backseat to counting as a measurement method in business. However, if counting is not possible, judging can be very useful in helping people improve. Many Olympic sports use judging very well and to the benefit of the performers.

Counting

When we can, we should count. In business, we are usually interested in the rate of doing something. We typically want to increase such things as quality parts per hour, sales per week, and customer inquiry calls completed per day. These things are usually thought of as easy to measure, but nothing is easy to measure if the performer doesn't want to be measured. If people don't want to be measured, they can find many reasons why what you have chosen to measure is not a valid indicator of their performance.

Raw Versus Cooked.   When you establish a measurement using counting, consider using the raw data rather than some mathematical function such as percent. Lindsley (1993) puts forth a convincing argument that percent correct or incorrect is the wrong measurement method for business because it is a way of "cooking the data." The further you move away from raw data, the more data you lose.

For example, he points out that percent change is not symmetrical: "many of us do not realize that if you add 20 percent and then subtract 20 percent, you are not back to where you started; you are actually below where you started." Typically used as a way of reporting such things as manufacturing efficiencies, yields, and quality, percent treats "corrects" and "incorrects" as dependent entities. In fact, they are independent of one another. As such, percent obscures some useful data. As an example, if someone produced 1,000 units with 100 defects, she would have 90 percent good parts and 10 percent errors. If the next day she produced 1,200 units and 110 were defects, she would have 90.8 percent good parts and 9.2 percent defects. Quality would appear to have improved, but, in fact, more defective units were produced. This could not be detected from the percent data.

By examining the raw frequencies (uncooked data), you might be able to spot a problem and correct it much earlier than if you had only percent measures. For example, Lindsley has discovered 11 patterns of correct and incorrect performance that can be detected by plotting responses. He calls these patterns "learning pictures." Seven of these are illustrated in Figure 11-1. By studying these pictures, you can see how corrects and incorrects are independent. Percentage does not add any new information and practically always masks useful data.

Percent can be particularly misleading if you don't know the frequency of the behavior being counted. One of something can be 100 percent and 100 of something can be 100 percent. If we don't know the actual frequency, we can't adequately evaluate performance. It's not unusual for a batter in professional baseball to carry a very high batting average early in the season, say, .667. Does this mean that he is a great hitter? You'd be cautious about declaring him the next Ted Williams if you knew he had only batted three times.

Use raw data where you can. It will give you more information, generate more hypotheses, and lead you to quicker resolution of problems than will percent.

Judging

Many things in business are not readily countable. This makes judging a very useful tool. The biggest problem with measures based on judging is that in many cases they appear to be arbitrary. What is being evaluated

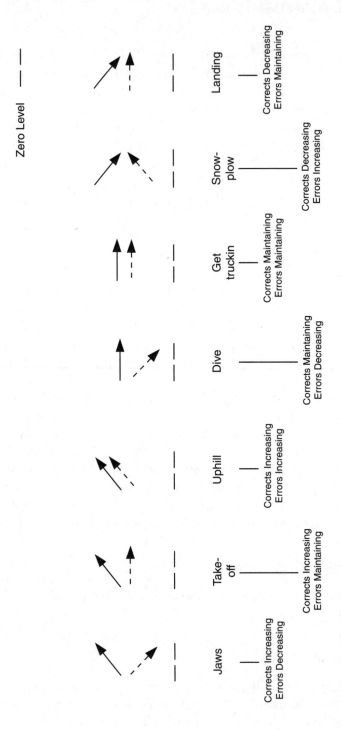

Figure 11-1 Lindsley's learning pictures.

seems to vary from one measurement to the next. A way of overcoming this problem is to establish specific criteria that can be reliably observed by two or more people. Many athletic events, such as gymnastics, ice skating, and diving, to name a few, rely on multiple judges and use their composite score to determine winners and losers, and for the most part, spectators and athletes accept the scores as valid.

The legal profession has long wrestled with the subjectivity of judging and seeks to build a body of evidence to assist in making decisions of guilt or innocence. In business, we can overcome the subjectivity of judging by constructing a *behaviorally anchored rating scale* (BARS). A BARS is a scale on which each variable to be measured is anchored by specific behaviors and accomplishments. Quality performance and customer service are two areas where studies employing BARS have been used to assist in the evaluation process. The scale is usually constructed by performers and their boss, or teams may construct one for themselves. Figure 11-2 is an example of a BARS. Remember, when measurement is used to provide opportunities for positive reinforcement, much of the criticism of judging is reduced.

Rate Not Rank.   One of the most frequently used measurement methods is ranking. I strongly advise against it. Ranking should not be used because it sets one employee against another. There can be only one number one and only a limited number of winners. We don't intentionally hire losers. Let's not use measurement to create them.

By using ratings, we compare performance against established criteria. In this way, it is possible for everyone who meets the required criteria to be rated as a top performer. A company of winners will be a winning company.

Validating Behavioral Measures

When measuring behavior, it is important to compare behavioral measures against results. If behaviors are judged to be good but the results are not, you have not pinpointed the critical behaviors for the results you are measuring. You should reinforce doing what was asked for, but you need to refine the behavioral pinpoints until they correlate highly with the desired results. Remember, the behaviors you originally pinpoint may have to be revised and/or refined a number of times until they give you the desired pinpointed result.

Behaviors: Perform required tests, identify problems, schedule repairs.

Performs **all** tests on **all** equipment as scheduled.

Identify **all** problems.

Coordinates assignments with repair supervisor.

weight _____
score _____

Performs no tests. Makes repair assignments based on past data. Turns over to repair supervisor with no discussion.
— (1)

Performs less than 50% of required tests on 75-100% of required equipment. Turns over to repair supervisor with no discussion.
— (3)

Performs 75-100% of required tests on 75-100% of required equipment on time. Turns over to repair supervisor with no discussion.
— (5)

Performs 100% of required tests on 100% of required equipment on time. Turns over to repair supervisor with no discussion.
— (7)

Performs 100% of required tests on 100% of required equipment on time. Discusses with repair supervisor before completing repair schedule.

Performs 100% of required tests on 100% of required equipment on time. Discusses with repair supervisor before completing repair schedule. Follows up to be sure work has been done as scheduled.

Performs 100% of required tests on 100% of required equipment on time. Discusses with repair supervisor before completing repair schedule. Follows up to be sure work has been done as scheduled. Identifies potential problems not on maintenance list.
— (10)

Scale: 1   3   5   7   10

Figure 11-2 Preventive maintenance technician.

A sales division of a grocery products company developed a checklist for salespeople to complete after every sales call. The checklist included items such as

1. Did I sell a promotion?
2. Did I ask for the order?
3. Did I ask for additional facings?
4. Did I cross-sell our new product?

The sales reps tallied their scores (0 or 1) for each customer and plotted them on a graph at the end of each day. At the end of the week, they sent the graph of their completed checklists to their supervisor. The sales supervisor also plotted each sales rep's scores on the checklist against "cases sold." He was pleasantly surprised to find a very high correlation between behaviors and results.

Because there was a high overall correlation, the scores helped to diagnose individual performance problems. If someone had high scores on the checklist and no increase in sales, it indicated that there might be a problem in how the person was setting up and conducting the sales call. During the time the division used this checklist and correlated behaviors with results, it experienced record sales.

In another case, an accounting manager wanted to focus on past-due accounts as a way of improving cash flow. He had two clerks who were working on this job. His checklist was called "Positive Credit Calls" and included only behaviors the clerks could control. To earn credit for a call, the clerks had to (1) find the name of a person in the company who could take action on the bill, (2) call and talk to that person, (3) get some form of commitment to take action on the bill, and (4) record the stated action on a log at his or her desk. The accounting manager then checked the number of calls against the number of past-due accounts that were paid each week. The clerks doubled the number of positive credit calls per day, and it resulted in an impressive improved cash flow.

Measurement Helps You See Small Changes

One of the most important reasons for establishing a good measurement system is to enable you to see small, incremental changes. Most improvements do not occur suddenly. Frequently, improvement has begun, and you hardly notice it. Many initiatives have been canceled when progress was under way, but there was no measurement system in place to let anybody know about it. Because American business is noted for its impatience and a desire for a "quick fix," having a way to measure small improvements is critical.

Years ago, I worked with a teacher who asked for help with a student who would suddenly yell out for no apparent reason. She told me she had him tested by the school psychologist, who diagnosed him as "having a need to scream." Don't we all! The teacher also told me that the student was driving her crazy. She never knew when he would yell.

"How often does he yell," I asked.

"All the time," she responded.

Knowing that he could not be yelling *all the time*, I asked her to record the number of times he yelled in class during the next week.

When I visited her the following week, even I was shocked by the data. He averaged yelling out once every six minutes—about 50 times a day. I suggested an intervention that she faithfully implemented.

Let us say that she obtained the following results:

Time frame	Yells per day
Baseline	52
Monday	49
Tuesday	48
Wednesday	46
Thursday	41
Friday	40

If you were the teacher and I asked you if the student was getting better, what would you say? The teacher said he was getting better. As a matter of fact, he did scream less every day.

"Do you think we should continue for another week?" I asked.

"Yes, of course," she responded.

Suppose for a moment that I told this teacher to try the same intervention *but didn't ask her to count the yells per day*. What do you think she would have told me the next week? I'm sure she would have said that there was no improvement, because, without measurement, the difference between screaming 52 times a day and 40 times a day probably would have gone unnoticed. Forty yells per day is still a lot of yells.

In case you were wondering, the intervention we used was to set a timer on the student's desk. For every 10 minutes he could go without yelling and working at his desk, he got to spend one minute with the teacher after school, a positive reinforcer for this student. This allowed the teacher to reward him a minimum of once every 10 minutes, and it allowed her to see progress at the same time. A good measurement system should provide reinforcement opportunities for both the measurer and the measuree.

By the way, at the end of the day on Friday of the first week, the student came to the teacher and said, "Next week, can I go 20 minutes without yelling?" By the end of the second week, he had stopped yelling and did not yell a single time during the rest of the year.

I'm sure I don't have to sell you on the importance of measurement in business. In business, we have to keep score. But measurement used to set the occasion for positive reinforcement has benefits that you may never have imagined. More than keeping score, measurement can add significantly to bringing out the best in people.

Notes

1. J. Kantor and D. Streitfeld, "Inside Amazon: Wrestling Big Ideas in a Bruising Workplace." *New York Times*, August 15, 2015.

12

Performance Feedback

Pinpointing defines the results you want and the behaviors you need to get them. Measurement tells you how much of each you are getting. Once you have those two performance management elements in place, you are ready to turn that information into feedback.

The term *feedback* is not to be confused with general information or data. *Feedback, as the term is used here, is information about performance that allows an individual to adjust his or her performance.* Feedback shows a performer where current performance is in relation to past performance and usually some goal.

Without feedback, there is no learning. You can't learn to talk, walk, write, ride a bicycle, or play a musical instrument without feedback. *Learning requires specific information about how your behavior is affecting the environment.*

For the most part, feedback is such an integral part of everyday life that we take it for granted. Our senses constantly provide us with information that helps us adjust our behavior in order to walk safely, type correctly, hammer a nail, fill a cup with coffee, or pick up the phone.

Although much of the feedback we experience in daily life is built into our biology and physiology, in most jobs we do not get the feedback we need to perform optimally. Ordinary performance data alone do not necessarily tell you what to do to improve performance. A golfer who sees a ball slice wildly from the tee into the woods certainly has information about performance but may not have the slightest idea what he or she did wrong. To this golfer, the information is not helpful—it's punishing. Because there are many things that cause a golf ball to slice, to the novice golfer, simply observing the ball careening off in the wrong direction is not helpful to his or her game. However, the consequence of having the ball go into the woods may eventually (or in some cases immediately) cause that individual to give up the game.

Similar situations exist in businesses, where industrially engineered standards may be so complex that beginning performers don't benefit from seeing these data. Performance feedback, by behavioral definition, is specific information or data about performance that will allow you to change or maintain your performance.

If you have an accounting job that involves invoicing customers, for example, there is nothing in the job that automatically causes you to adjust the pace or the accuracy of your work. When there is no naturally occurring feedback, some mechanism must be developed by which this kind of information is generated and presented to the performer. Performers need to know how they are doing, whether they should pick up the pace, slow down, or be more careful.

In his lectures on improving quality, Dr. W. Edwards Deming repeatedly asked, "How could they know?" He was referring to the sad fact that most performers do not receive or have access to the feedback they need to do a quality job.

Feedback deficiencies are a major contributor to virtually all problems of low performance, yet most organizations today have no real system for providing performance feedback to their employees. Even companies that are now sharing production figures or quality indicators with employees are typically providing information, not feedback. This kind of information gives performers only a vague idea of how they are doing. It has little impact on their job performance. With effective feedback, improvements ranging from 20 to 600 percent aren't unusual!

Feedback Is an Antecedent

Once again, I must point out that feedback is very important, but alone it will not sustain behavior change. In a large number of documented cases, performance has doubled in a short period of time following the introduction of performance feedback. This causes many managers to think that feedback produces some kind of performance magic. However, they are often disappointed when several weeks or even days later the performance drops to prefeedback levels.

The surge in performance occurs because feedback is an antecedent for behavior change, and you'll recall that effective antecedents can get almost any behavior to start. Feedback tells the performer what needs to change in his or her performance. How the performers choose to respond to that antecedent depends on the consequences they experience, have experienced, or expect to experience.

Feedback Doesn't Always Improve Performance

It is possible that for some performers feedback could be an antecedent to limit their performance. They may be afraid that they will run out of work and lose their jobs, or they may be concerned that feedback will illustrate their superior work, causing other workers to be jealous. Peer pressure is a powerful consequence and usually not positive.

In a performance management system, improving performance is an occasion for positive reinforcement. Feedback is an excellent format for the performer and the manager to know when positive reinforcement is due. The reinforcement for the behavior that is associated with the feedback is necessary to sustain the performance improvement.

Feedback in Graphs

Although feedback is technically defined here as any information about performance that will allow you to change that performance, in this chapter I am going to emphasize feedback presented in graphic format. Graphed data have many advantages over charts, text, or data presented verbally.

Graphs show you at a glance where you are in relation to where you have been and where you are going. Graphed data allow you to see performance trends earlier, permitting a more timely response to potential problems and more immediate positive reinforcement.

Dean Tapp, consultant to a label-printing company, reports a case where press operators were given verbal feedback in an effort to increase sheets per hour on printing jobs. Verbal feedback, given by the supervisor, on current performance (usually given the following day) sounded something like this: "You ran 14,156 sheets per hour yesterday." As you can see

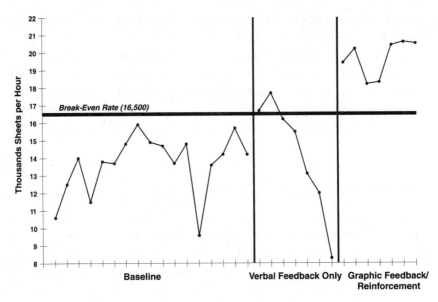

Figure 12-1   Sheets per hour.

from Figure 12-1, performance deteriorated. As you will recognize, verbal feedback was actually a punisher because it caused performance to decrease. When the company began using systematic graphic feedback and reinforcement, performance improved dramatically.

Feedback Interval

Obviously, immediate feedback on performance is preferred. With immediate and frequent feedback, people learn more quickly because they are provided more opportunities for reinforcement than less frequent, more delayed feedback would permit. Many managers and supervisors say that it's impossible to provide immediate feedback.

The question I ask in such circumstances is, "Then what is the shortest practical interval?" Hourly feedback is better than daily feedback, and daily feedback is preferable to weekly feedback. Feedback delivered less often than weekly is better than nothing, but not much better. Most activity trackers, such as Fitbit, owe their popularity to the fact that the person can get instantaneous feedback. Monthly feedback is much too delayed to have any significant impact on performance. After all, monthly feedback only provides 11 opportunities a year to reinforce or correct performance.

Daily feedback is the most common feedback interval in most performance management applications. Daily feedback is possible on more jobs than you might imagine. Employees on production jobs, office jobs, and even creative jobs such as software development can easily arrange a system for daily feedback. Once again, I am referring to graphic feedback. Using graphs makes frequent feedback possible.

Individual Versus Group Feedback

Individual feedback is more effective than group feedback. As you might imagine, managers will say, "I can't get data by individual performer." If you can't do it, don't do it. But get it for the smallest group possible.

When you have individual feedback, you should graph group performance as well. This provides increased opportunities for reinforcement for the individuals in the group while increasing reinforcement opportunities for cooperation and other teamwork behaviors.

Public or Private. Post group performance grafts publicly; provide individual feedback privately. We encourage individuals to keep a notebook of their performance and show it to their supervisors daily. This gives the supervisor the opportunity to reinforce, if appropriate, and offer help, if needed. This is a powerful way to maximize performance.

Supervisors should keep individual performance data private. Resist the temptation to compare one performer with another. Don't say, "Courtney completed 123 documents yesterday, and I know that you can do as well." This sets Courtney up as a punisher to the others and does not foster teamwork. However, if a person asks, "How many did Courtney do yesterday?" the proper response is, "Ask Courtney." Voluntarily sharing feedback among peers offers many opportunities for peer reinforcement.

In an organization where measurement is being used to provide positive reinforcement, it is not unusual for individuals to post their own graphs publicly. If they choose to do so, great, but don't ask them to do it. Remember, public recognition can be punishing for some people, and you could be setting up a negative-reinforcement situation if you post individual graphs when the performers would rather you didn't.

Sales organizations often publish a newsletter or memo ranking each salesperson. Just because this is frequently done doesn't mean that it's an effective procedure. I strongly discourage this practice. Listing the names of those above goal is a preferred alternative. A graph showing the highest performance (without naming the performer) and the average and lowest performances (again without the names) will produce the same results as ranking, without the negative side effects.

However, always publish group results publicly. When group graphs are posted publicly, it often increases reinforcement between members of the group and also encourages positive remarks from visitors in the work area.

Performer-Controlled Feedback

Just as with pinpointing and measurement, don't give feedback on variables that are not under the control of the individual or the group. There is no advantage to be gained, and it may be frustrating for the performers if you post a graph over which they have little or no control.

I recall an incident in the production area of a furniture manufacturing plant. The plant manager pointed to a huge graph on the wall and said, "Here is our feedback graph." I looked at it and noticed that there was no apparent trend, so I asked, "How are you doing?"

He replied, "Good!"

I pointed to a high point on the graph and said, "Boy, you knocked the top out this day, didn't you?"

"Naw," he responded, "We worked 10 hours that day."

"What happened here?" I asked as I pointed to the low point on the graph.

"We had some equipment problems that day," he replied.

Contrary to what the plant manager thought, this graph was not feedback to the production employees. It may have been feedback to the production controller, production superintendent, and plant manager—but not to the line employees. The line employees needed feedback on the number of chairs they finished per hour when the line was running. That way, they could see the difference their pace and skill made. The graph being used did not help individuals improve their performance. By the way, a large production graph in the plant is a good idea. Even though this particular graph was not performance feedback for the employees, with the addition of group and individual feedback, as well as controllable variables, it could become a source of reinforcement and reward for the general plant population.

I saw a second example of a performer-control error in another furniture plant. In this case, management was concerned about the amount of money being spent on sandpaper. One manager organized a work team to reduce the dollars spent on sandpaper. The team worked really hard for a month, coming up with many ideas and implementing them successfully.

The group was stunned when, at the end of the month, they saw that *the amount of money spent for sandpaper had essentially stayed the same.* It turned out that the vendor had two price increases for sandpaper that month. No amount of explaining by the manager could offset the disappointment the group felt when members saw no change in the costs they worked so hard to reduce.

The manager could have assured success if he had given feedback on "increasing board feet per sandpaper belt." That was something the workers could control.

Feedback and Reinforcement

Feedback and positive reinforcement form the most powerful combination of techniques you can use to bring out the best in people. To have effective feedback, you must have the right pinpoints. Then add feedback and reinforcement, and you will have the right mix to maximize performance.

The plant manager of a company based in St. Paul, Minnesota, recently told me that as he posted record group data on a plant graph, one of the most militant union members walked by, saw the graph, and shouted, "Alright!" as he threw his fist up in the air. "Seeing such a change in that man made all the effort in using performance management worthwhile," the manager said with a big smile.

To be most effective, feedback must be established as an antecedent for positive reinforcement. Although performance feedback is not a natural reinforcer, when performers know that positive reinforcement is consistently paired with improved performance, simply watching the graphed data move in the right direction can become a source of considerable reinforcement.

13

A Model for Problem Solving

The Model

All the individual elements necessary to bring out the best in people must be applied in a systematic format for solving performance problems and maximizing performance. In the early 1960s, Ogden Lindsley (1991) developed such a model and used it effectively in his work with parents, teachers, and students. He wanted a way of solving problems that would be simple for parents to use and to teach to their children.

The original model was composed of four steps

1. Pinpoint

2. Record

3. Consequate

4. Evaluate

I modified Lindsley's model slightly for use in business. I divided the second step, Record, into the substeps of Measure and Feedback, and changed "Consequate" to "Reinforce." The resulting model looks this:

1. Pinpoint

2. Measure

3. Feedback

4. Reinforce

5. Evaluate

Differences in these two versions are slight. Lindsley asked the people he worked with to record their data on six-cycle log paper (called a *standard celeration chart*), which would automatically give them a graphic display, a rate, and a trend of their data. He used the six-cycle chart because he observed that learning multiplies and the log paper is a multiply chart, so it provides a more accurate account of learning than the usual add chart. However, if I had asked frontline supervisors and managers to record data on a log chart in addition to everything else I asked them to do, I knew that they'd kick me out of their companies.

Another slight difference in the two models is the word *consequate*. Lindsley coined this word to mean simply that there should be an application of consequences—positive or negative. My original thought was that managers don't need to be told to punish more but should be encouraged to find solutions that are positively reinforcing.

Because business is interested in increasing performance, I knew that reinforcement had to be the emphasis. Because of this, some people mistakenly think that punishment is not a part of performance management. Punishment is a consequence that does have a place in managing performance, as I pointed out earlier. Yet, when you use positive consequences correctly, you'll find that punishment begins to play a smaller and smaller role in your management activity.

The power of the performance management problem-solving model lies in its systematic use. You can't use the pinpointing technique alone and expect to get any lasting change. You can't measure and then use it as a way to punish. You can't give feedback without reinforcement and expect to see sustained improvement. You can't even reinforce without the other steps because, if you do, you will probably reinforce the wrong behaviors at the wrong time. The problem-solving model starts with pinpointing and ends with evaluation for an important reason. All steps must be used, in that order, to take full advantage of the power of the model to improve performance.

One of the most important actions for management is to *positively reinforce the behavior of those who use the model* to improve performance. Don't wait until employees get improved performance (a result). "Using the model" to solve problems or improve performance at work is a reinforceable behavior.

This Model Works on *All* Performance Problems

One of the main obstacles I have encountered over the years when trying to get companies to use this behavioral model as the total way to approach their business is the reaction that "it's too simple for our complex problems." The model is simple. Applying it is not.

This model applies to any aspect of business—from downsizing to cycle time reduction. If you need to increase sales, this model works. If you need more new products from the lab, this model works.

Dr. Glenn Latham, a retired behavior analyst at Utah State University, stated in his article "The Application of Behaviorological Principles":

> It is my experience that eventually, reasonable, honest, and effective solutions can be found *for every single problem. No exceptions!* I have become absolutely unequivocal and fearless on that point, so much so that I am willing to bet anyone $10,000 that, relative to any behavioral problem, if they will be honest about it, and do what I tell them to do, an effective intervention will be found and within a reasonable period of time.

Implementing the Model

To implement this model, you must select a pinpoint and begin measurement prior to a performance intervention. This allows you to collect a baseline, a starting point, against which you can evaluate the effect of the intervention. In performance management, an *intervention* is typically defined as the introduction of systematic feedback and reinforcement.

If you evaluate your results and see that your intervention of systematic feedback and reinforcement is not working, you should reexamine the reinforcer step to determine whether the consequence you are providing is really a reinforcer to the recipient(s). If the behavior is changing but the result is not, you have probably selected the wrong pinpoint. In any event, to be successful, you must complete all the steps of the model. If you don't get the results you want, change one element at a time, and monitor your results—the same procedure a scientist follows—until you solve the problem. Most of the problems in applying the model are that the critical behaviors have not been pinpointed or what was chosen as a positive reinforcer is not one. Solving these problems may require two or three iterations of the model.

Can We Do Science at Work?

The model described in this chapter lends itself to scientific analysis. Because of the precision of the pinpointing, measurement, and intervention, you can easily measure pre- and postintervention performance. Then you can use one of several research designs to evaluate the effects of your performance management intervention.

Evaluating the Impact of a Performance Management Intervention

B Design

In this evaluation design, you decide what you want to do to change performance, you do it, and then you track the results. B is the intervention. Most people in business are content if things get better. However, this is the least powerful design for testing whether your intervention was responsible for any change. This approach is weak because you have no baseline against which you can evaluate your intervention (Figure 13-1).

AB Design

This design requires that you collect baseline data on current performance before you intervene. These data allow you to show that the performance

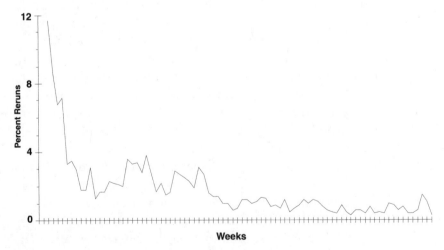

Figure 13-1   B design: Reruns as a percent of completed jobs.

was not moving in the right direction until after the intervention. Then, if improvement starts after your intervention, you have some evidence that your intervention is responsible for the change. A critic could claim (and often will) that the improvement was due to another change in the working conditions that occurred simultaneously with your intervention. They point to environmental, economic, seasonal, or other such changes to explain the differences. Although this test is more powerful than the B design, it's still considered relatively weak as far as scientific proof is concerned (Figure 13-2).

ABA Design

This is a more powerful design than either the B or AB design because it involves a return to baseline conditions, the final A. For example, if your intervention consisted of introducing some form of reinforcement and *after a period of time, you withdraw the reinforcement to see if the performance returns to its previous baseline level.*

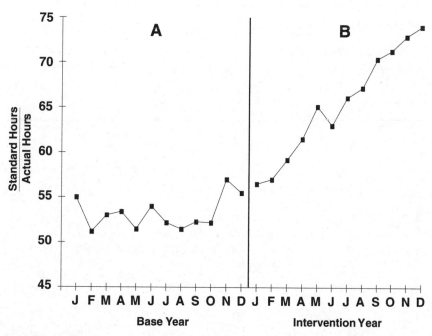

Figure 13-2   AB design: Aerospace fastener manufacturer productivity improvement.

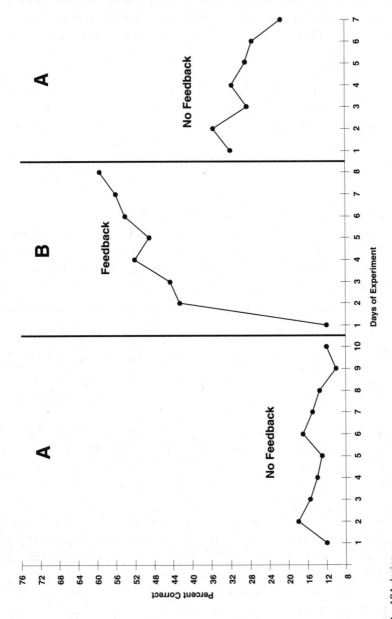

Figure 13-3 ABA design.

The problem with this design is that a manager in an ongoing business would rarely want to stop something that is working just to prove that the intervention is really the cause of the improvement (Figure 13-3).

Multiple-Baseline Design

A multiple-baseline design is several AB designs implemented at varied times. This is one of the most powerful designs because you can do as many AB designs as you need to determine cause and effect. This is easy to do and, in my opinion, should be standard operating procedure with any new program or initiative in order to evaluate its effectiveness (Figure 13-4).

All these evaluation designs can be applied in the workplace. I call them *noninvasive*. This means that you do not have to disrupt the normal conduct of business to test the efficacy of your intervention.

The usual social science and psychological model requires that you set up control and experimental groups. This means that you balance the two groups on all variables (i.e., age, sex, education, experience, etc.) that might affect the outcome. It also usually requires that you either set up an artificial situation or that you reassign people. As you might imagine, very little of this type of research is done in real work situations. The designs described in this chapter use the group (or individual) as its own control, eliminating the need for any change that could be disruptive or nonproductive.

Once again, this method should be standard operating procedure for evaluating any effort to change any aspect of performance. If this approach is used routinely, it *will* save organizations millions of dollars over the years by eliminating commonsense solutions that don't work but are not usually evaluated.

Hopkins and colleagues (1992) suggest that there are so many ineffective strategies being sold to businesses that some sort of business protection agency needs to be formed "to protect vulnerable and unwitting corporate and agency executives from unscrupulous or unwitting social scientists, consultants, and personnel staff members who promise salvation but, in fact, deliver unproven and possibly completely useless or even harmful technology."

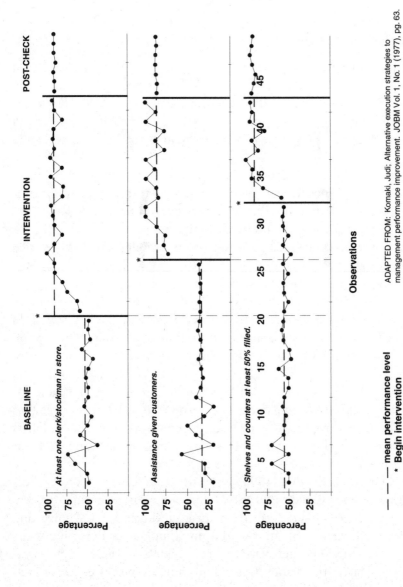

Figure 13-4 Multiple-baseline design.

ADAPTED FROM: Komaki, Judi; Alternative execution strategies to management performance improvement. JOBM Vol. 1, No. 1 (1977), pg. 63.

PART 4

Turning Good Intentions into High Performance

14

Goal Setting to Shape Behavior

Make haste slowly.

—BENJAMIN FRANKLIN

Few things consume more management time than goal setting. Establishing "realistic, attainable, yet challenging goals" has been a battle cry for legions of managers—and management consultants. In fact, training courses in goal setting and the accompanying "conducting an effective performance appraisal meeting" are second only to sales management skills as the most popular nontechnical training courses offered by most companies.

You'd think that as often as goals are discussed, developed, and used by managers, there would be agreement on how to set goals and document their value to business. Yet there is not. *SMART* goals are very popular today, I think, because the acronym is easy to remember. SMART stands for **s**pecific, **m**easurable, **a**chievable, **r**esults, and **t**ime-bound.

Can you see what's missing? It should be obvious by now. There are no consequences in the model, positive or negative. In other words, they are not very smart. Although I do not have specific research on these SMART goals, I would bet that they are not any more effective than traditional goals because the same feature is missing from them as well.

As I've mentioned previously, noted quality expert W. Edwards Deming advised us to eliminate goals and standards altogether. Deming had observed how, in actual practice, goals and standards limit performance. He said that people who are capable of more reach their goal level and stop. In other words, performers typically give only what is asked for, even when they are capable of more.

Remember, in earlier chapters I described this same scenario as a sign of management by negative reinforcement. What Deming saw in many organizations was that the majority of people attain goals in order to escape or avoid the consequences of not meeting the goals rather than attaining or exceeding their goals as a means of receiving positive reinforcement.

Understanding the True Nature of Goals

Goals are antecedents for either reinforcement or punishment. If people are punished when they fail to reach a goal, they will reach the goal, if they can, only to avoid the punishment. However, if people reach their goals and receive positive reinforcement, they will not stop when they get to goal but will continue to perform at their best, knowing that more positive reinforcement will be forthcoming.

The belief that goals improve performance interferes with their effective use. If goals are set but there are no consequences for either success or failure, the goals will produce no improvement and ultimately will be a waste of time.

A textile sales organization in New York used a goal-setting process called *targeting* with its salespeople. This semiannual process consumed several months of management time each year. It involved the sales manager sitting with each salesperson, reviewing every account, and setting sales targets for the next sales season.

When asked how many targets were met each season, the most common response by far was "about 75 percent." The actual data were available but were not routinely reviewed. When we actually examined results for the previous season, we discovered that only 8 percent of the targets had actually been met! Management was shocked and was sure that the data were wrong. We then looked at the data from the season before and found that goal attainment was only 11 percent.

Management had mistakenly assumed that good participative goal setting would surely produce improvement.

Goals Get Results (A Management Myth)

What we know by now is that the setting event will not produce the outcome if the consequences don't favor it. Goals, no matter how well conceived, are antecedents. Only if they are antecedents for positive reinforcement will people be enthusiastic about reaching them and willing to set more.

The Best Mistake

When Deming encouraged management to eliminate goal setting, he was really calling for the *elimination of goals as they are currently used*. And I agree. However, I know that goal setting does have the potential to contribute to improved performance if used in the correct way.

Very clearly, *the purpose of setting goals should be to increase opportunities for positive reinforcement. If this is the purpose, we should want many, not few, goals.* And contrary to common sense, the best mistake to make in goal setting is to *set the goals too low*. The reasons for these techniques may be obvious to you by now:

1. If the goal is low, it increases the probability of success. If the goal is reached *and success is celebrated*, the motivation to do even more the next time is increased. It is not far-fetched to expect goals to be set where attainment is 100 percent. This will ramp up faster than larger goals and exceed them more often.

2. If goals become the antecedent for positive reinforcement, then the more goals you have, the more occasions there are for positive reinforcement.

The mistake that is most commonly made when setting goals is associated with the word *challenging*. The concept of "challenging goals" usually causes managers to set fewer goals and to set them too high. Fewer goals that are harder to attain mean very few opportunities for positive reinforcement and reward. The result is a lower number of goals attained.

The Challenge of Stretch Goals

I hope by this time that your company has discontinued the practice of setting *stretch* goals. Stretch goals reduce the probability of success because they are too difficult, maybe even impossible, to attain. "Stretching" reduces the probability of success. Depending on how far your performers are stretching, the probability of success may be less than 50 percent. No business can survive these days by reaching its goals only 50 percent of the time. Researchers have observed that fewer than 10 percent of stretch goals are ever reached.

Stretch goals evolved as a means of avoiding the phenomenon Deming observed. That is, people get to the goal and wait for the next one before starting to improve again. When there is a goal and then a stretch goal beyond the initial one, people know they can't quit, but they also know that failing to reach the stretch goal won't be "the end of the world" because management is admitting that the probability of attainment is low. Using stretch goals to try to fool people into superior performance just doesn't work.

As I mentioned previously, when I talk negatively about stretch goals, I annoy many managers because they have used them and consider them successful, although they rarely have any data on attainment rate. Rather than being annoyed, they should be excited about the possibilities that using better methods provide.

Make Haste Slowly

You may have gotten the idea that when I say things like "set goals that are relatively easy to achieve," I don't understand the urgent demand for dramatic improvement in the marketplace today. To the contrary, I understand that the urgency is so great that we can't afford any more mistakes in the use of goals and standards, whether applied to individuals or to the organization as a whole. We can't afford to waste another decade guessing about goal setting. We can't afford to waste another day. Let's stop guessing and look at what we know.

Equal Goals Are Unfair to All

Nothing is more unequal than the equal treatment of unequals.
      —Attributed to Vince Lombardi

Across-the-board goals are unfair to everybody. For example, if we ask for 10 percent improvement in productivity from everybody, it will generally be too difficult for the lowest performers, too easy for the average performers, and too difficult for the best performer.

The learning curve in Figure 14-1 illustrates the proper way to set goals. At the lower end of the curve, notice that the goals are modest. In the middle range, the goals are more moderate. At the upper end, the goals are once again smaller. Lindsley (1991), mentioned earlier, taught that all goals should be equally difficult.

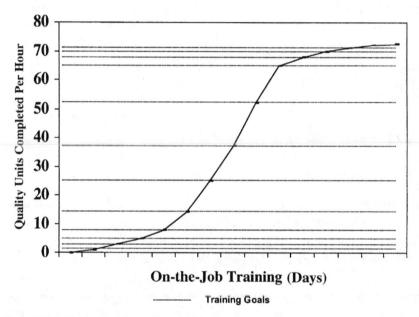

On-the-Job Training (Days)

————— **Training Goals**

Figure 14-1 Goal setting in a training situation.

Look at it this way: if the average performer can do 100 units per hour, a 10 percent improvement would be 110, an increase of 10 units. For performers completing only 80 per hour, this seems equitable, an increase of only 8, but the problem is that if doing more were easy, they would already be doing more. Because they are behind every day, the organizational consequences and consequences from the supervisor are typically not positive, but yet they still don't do more. On the other end of the scale, those doing 120 per hour have to do 132 just to meet the goal, an increase of 12. The problem is that because the top-end performers are close to the asymptote, any improvement is difficult.

For each performer, you should set the first goal slightly ahead of his or her current performance. You will make much more progress if you use short time-frames (i.e., days, weeks) and smaller goals than you will if you set high goals and longer time-frames (i.e., month, quarter, year).

The process of setting attainable goals based on current performance allows you to reinforce everyone for his or her individual performance. It also allows all performers to progress at their own pace.

Take the case of an individual in a group performing at 73 units per day when he should be at 110 per day. Don't hesitate to start with an initial goal of 75, even if others in the group are producing at much higher levels. The next goal might be 77 or 78 and the next after that 83 or 85.

If you use daily or weekly goals, it won't take long for a reinforced performer to reach the ultimate goal; when he gets there, you will have a turned-on, fired-up individual. Compare this approach with one where you tell the entire work group that everybody needs to produce at 110, 120, or more and then wait until they do before you provide any reinforcement. You might wait a long time.

Slow and Steady Wins the Race—More than a Fable

The *fastest* way to change individual behavior is to set small goals, reinforce effort, and celebrate attainment. Remember, positive reinforcement accelerates the rate of improvement. The only way we can achieve dramatic improvement in anything is with lots of reinforcement.

Think about your organization. Think about yourself. If you can't visualize how you and the rest of management are going to act when the organization is successful, you will probably not be in a position to celebrate effectively when you are. The Japanese have a saying, "Many raindrops make an ocean." This means that every improvement, no matter how small, is valuable and a cause for some recognition.

Americans seem to have a hard time with this. We want large, rapid changes, and we want them now! Our motto seems to be, "If you can't give me want I want right now, I will get someone who can."

Well, that approach is a trap. The resources to make dramatic change are most likely already at your fingertips. Consider this: suppose that you have 1,000 people in your company. At the end of the day, as everybody is leaving, you ask them, "Tomorrow, do you think you could do your job this much better?" as you hold your index finger and thumb a quarter inch apart. What do you think people will say? The overwhelming majority will say, "Sure!"

Let's say all 1,000 say, "Yes" and then actually make some small improvement. And you, in some way, let them know that you noticed and appreciated the improvement. At the end of the next workday you ask the same question. You will probably get another "Yes." How many days would you have to do this before the company's performance improved dramatically? Three weeks? A month? Surely not longer, because you would be compounding 1,000 improvements every day.

Think many small improvements; think frequent positive reinforcement.

Shaping: The Fastest Way to Change

The fastest way to improve performance actually seems slow. It involves positively reinforcing small improvements. Because positive reinforcement increases the rate of behavior by reinforcing small changes in performance, you are able to accelerate performance early and often.

If we reinforced every behavior in a learning situation, we would generate a lot more excitement, enthusiasm, and improvement than if we reinforced only every 100 behaviors. The *rate of change* is directly related to the number of reinforcers received.

The technical name for this process is *shaping*. *Shaping is the process of positively reinforcing successive approximations (small) toward a goal.* The ability to shape behavior is the essence of effective teaching, coaching, managing, and supervising. Shaping is at the heart of bringing out the best in people. To shape effectively requires the ability to break down a task into small steps, the patience to reinforce very small changes, and the celebration of reaching the final goal.

Creating Rubik's Fanatics

Years ago, I used to demonstrate how I could teach everybody to do the Rubik's cube, a popular three-dimensional puzzle. All I needed to "hook" them was 30 minutes with their hands on the cube. It was easy. I was able to generate so much enthusiasm with this shaping exercise that, eventually, I had to give it up as a classroom exercise because the class became so involved in practicing the cube that they couldn't focus on the class work.

The way I created this enthusiasm was first to teach the students how to find the "top" of the cube. I showed them how to determine the top, tossed it to them, and asked them to find it themselves. A simple verbal reinforcer, "Good," was sufficient to let them know they were successful. I repeated this process again and again until they were always successful at finding the top quickly. Then I showed them the next step of finding the colored blocks that should go on the top, then how to move those blocks to the top, and so on. Using this step-by-step approach, I arranged for them to receive several hundred reinforcers in 30 minutes. This was enough to keep many of them awake late into the night, practicing. The next morning they showed up early to ask my help with a step they couldn't remember, always eager to learn the next step.

I liked this problem as a class exercise because moving the sides of the Rubik's cube is about as meaningless a task as you can devise. And when you're successful, the only thing to do is mess it up and start over again. It clearly demonstrates how *meaning resides in consequences—not behavior.*

The result of a completed cube was too far away from the initial tasks to provide any meaningful reinforcement. *It was only the many positive consequences that were provided for making one block at a time go into place that not only kept the students working on the cube in class but also induced them to continue to work on it for hours into the evening.*

The example of shaping that I have just described may sound impractical for the real world of work. In fact, however, it is very pragmatic and efficient. It requires only two things: (1) the final outcome must be important to you and/or the company, and (2) there must be positive reinforcement for very small increments of change.

If the change is important, it is worth the investment of your time. And if you will invest the time and effort in reinforcing often in the early stages of improvement, you will have to reinforce much less often later on. In other words, it takes a lot of reinforcement to establish a habit, but only an occasional reinforcer to keep it going.

You have probably heard the expression, "Pay me now or pay me later." The effective use of shaping costs you more time and effort now but will pay you many dividends in improved performance and reduction in turnover and in retraining time and disciplinary action later.

Organizational Goals and Benchmarking

IQS Study Explained

The International Quality Study (IQS, 1992) commissioned by the American Quality Foundation found that *benchmarking*, the practice of tracking business processes considered to be the best in a given sphere of influence ("best in industry" or "best in the world," for example), produced positive results on bottom-line variables only in the best-performing companies. Companies rated medium or low in performance showed no performance improvement. The study showed that "in fact, low performers who benchmark their marketing and sales systems can actually expect their performance to suffer."

When you understand how the average company uses goal setting, it is easy to see why the IQS found such results. The best-performing companies probably find the levels of performance of the benchmark companies to be easily attainable. As such, they could get a lot of reinforcement from the knowledge that attainable improvement resulted in being on track to be the "best in the world," "best in the industry," and so on.

However, many of the medium and low performers probably were overwhelmed by the gap between their performance and that of the benchmark. Indeed, some managers probably used the data to punish low performers.

These lower-performing companies must focus first on incremental gains with small goals. This will increase confidence in their ability to improve. As small gains are made, the subsequent gains will be bigger and bigger. Soon these companies will be in a position to compete with, even challenge, the best companies in the world.

Remember, where you set goals in relation to present performance is critical, but the most important thing is the celebration of goal attainment. The celebration of attainment is what makes goals motivating.

David McClelland, a Harvard psychologist, has studied achievement for many years. His research determined that the highest achievers in our society set *moderate* goals. Being the highest achievers probably means that they have high *aims* but that they use moderate goals to manage their performance day to day. Your employees are no different. They can and will operate at their best every day. What we have to do is help them to get to that point one step at a time. Asking for quantum leaps in performance will only discourage the performer and disappoint the manager who is asking. Goals can play a part in bringing out the best in people, but only when they are used as opportunities to recognize progress toward being the best.

15

The Four R's of Effective Management

Recognition, Reward, Reinforcement, and Relationships

There Are Cheaper Ways to Make People Unhappy

Few organizations are satisfied with their reward and recognition systems. Furthermore, every change in these systems results in someone else becoming unhappy. Most often management becomes cynical because no matter what it tries, "Nobody is satisfied." Every rule or process makes someone unhappy. Either the person who is subject to the rule or process or the person who developed the rule or process is unhappy because people won't follow him or her as they ought to.

Reward and recognition systems have changed little in the last 50 years. The only things that have changed about them are the size and type of reward or recognition. Companies are almost never able to prove that they get a motivational, morale, or bottom-line benefit from such systems. Yet almost no one is willing to abandon them because they feel that there must be a benefit somewhere.

Before proceeding further, some definitions are needed:

Recognition. Usually a symbolic way of showing appreciation for some accomplishment (including plaques, trophies, and letters of commendation). By its very nature, recognition is delayed and infrequent (positive, future, and uncertain [PFU]).

Reward. A tangible item, usually money or something exchangeable for money, that is intended to influence behavior in a particular direction. Because most rewards are not tailored to the person receiving them, it is not surprising that they do not motivate everyone. Because most rewards are for results, without regard to the behavior used to obtain them, it should not surprise anyone that people will try to get rewards with behaviors other than those desired. The fact that people will lie, cheat, and steal to get some rewards is not the fault of the rewards, but the fault of those who designed the system that allows those behaviors to be rewarded. Because rewards are always delayed, it is possible that the behaviors that triggered the reward may not be occurring when the reward is received, which inadvertently reinforces the wrong behavior (PFU).

Incentive. Used as an inducement to perform. The term as conventionally used is synonymous with reward but has often been used for recognition as well.

Bribe. For many parents, the terms *reward* and *bribe* are synonymous. In practice, they are very different. Rewards, for all the problems associated with their use, are delivered after some worthy accomplishment (a good thing). Bribes, however, are delivered before the accomplishment. To say "I will give you $10 to vote for my candidate" is a bribe, and a reward for some illegal activity is also considered a bribe. As you have read by now, a bribe or a reward for unsavory behavior is not a part of this process. It is not bribery to tell your child, "If you pass your math test next week, I will give you $10." It is simply a contingency. This is a reward, and there is nothing unsavory about the process. It may not be the most effective use of $10, but done the proper way, it may be effective and in no way will it harm the child.

Not everyone believes that rewards are a good thing. Parents often voice concern over rewarding their children for behaviors that they should be doing already. Safety experts have concern about rewarding employees for being safe for fear that they will cover up or not report accidents or unsafe behavior. Some retail businesses advertise that they don't pay commission on sales so that customers will know that they won't be pressured by a commissioned salesperson to buy something they don't really need or want.

In his book, *Punished by Rewards* (Houghton Mifflin, 1993), Alfie Kohn denigrates rewards. He generally equates them with bribes and states that they should not be used. His book was well read and his lectures well attended. Although he claimed that his book was based on research, he extrapolated considerably beyond the studies he quoted. However, the attention that he got, particularly from the business audience, is an indication of the dissatisfaction with current reward systems and the desperate attempts to find a better way. The rapid growth of the National Association for Employee Recognition (now Recognition Professionals International [RPI]) is also an indication of the interest in making them more effective.

You might ask if I am saying that rewards and recognition are bad for business and other organizations. I'm not saying that at all. When they are properly designed and implemented, they can have positive effects on an organization. When they are not, they are bad for employees and the organization, and most of the time they are not well designed and implemented.

Formal recognition and reward programs are often a substitute for a culture of engagement where relationships are seen as primary for a high-performance organization. Reward and recognition programs have at best short-term effects; however, when used in a reinforcement culture, the effects can be maintained.

Why is it that something that is so central to the way we do business is so problematic? In my opinion, this comes about because these systems are built from a commonsense and/or financial perspective rather than from a scientific understanding of how motivation works. For this reason, I think that most of them should be abandoned because a bad one is worse than none at all.

The recognition and rewards systems used by most organizations have one thing in common: the recognition and/or reward comes long after the behavior has occurred. As pointed out several times previously, any time there is a delay between the behavior and the consequence, there are potential problems. An annual recognition day where employees sit and watch a fraction of their peers get "recognition" is motivating to very few.

Where large cash awards, expensive prizes, or any form of tangible recognition is given to a limited number of individuals, the recognition program probably will demotivate more employees than it will motivate.

In addition, because these awards come so long after the accomplishment, it may appear to employees that management is uninformed about who really was responsible for the accomplishments. Frequently, large numbers of employees are left wondering why they weren't singled out for recognition when they worked as hard or harder than the people being recognized.

For now, I'm going to describe the problems with various commonly used forms of recognition and reward systems and suggest ways to overcome them.

Whether with rewards or recognition, the stated purpose among some executives is to have a program or system that will make positive examples of a few employees, which will cause others to work hard to achieve the same. However, most systems limit the number of employees who can get the reward or award at the same time. The words *first*, *most*, and *most improved* limit the number of people who actually receive the consequence. The words *top 5*, *top 10*, and *top 100* are worse. Here are a number of commonly used and ineffective recognition and reward procedures and programs.

Employee of the Month

People often ask me what I think of employee-of-the-month (EOM) programs. My advice to companies that have the standard EOM program is to eliminate it as quickly and as painlessly as possible. It won't be painless because some employees will express dissatisfaction with the termination because they didn't receive the award before it was terminated.

EOM is the most popular form of recognition in this country. Unfortunately, this form of recognition violates practically every known principle of effective recognition and positive reinforcement.

These programs do not specify precisely what must be done to get the award; they do not recognize performance immediately or frequently; they assume that the same form of recognition is desired by all; winning usually disqualifies the winner for getting the award again; and most troublesome, they allow for only one or at most a few winners.

EOM programs represent a very simplistic approach to the significant problem of employee motivation and human performance. While the goal of these programs is to recognize outstanding performance so that employees will feel better about their jobs, themselves, and the company, more often than not they accomplish the opposite because winning subjects the winners to peer ridicule or isolation.

Pinpointing Error

Employees generally do not understand what the EOM program is really about. The next time you see a plaque in a hotel or restaurant, ask an employee to explain it. At best, the employee will tell you something vague about hard work and good attitude. At last count, I had asked 77 people at various establishments, "What do you have to do to earn that?" Not one was able to tell me the criteria. The most common answer by far was, "I don't really know." One said, "Make more friends, I guess."

The answer that probably got closest to the truth came from a woman who worked at a rental car agency. She said, after a couple of minutes of reciting the company line, "I guess be nice to your manager."

Delay Error

The fact that most of the EOM plaques you see are often months out of date certainly says a lot about how important management thinks these programs are. Why an organization would publicly advertise its lack of importance is beyond me. You would think that such organizations would at least take the plaque down until it was brought up to date. But even the most up-to-date program is way too late. An award given once a month, even if all other elements were done well, still would not affect performance.

Just imagine that you have chosen your employee of the month because of some very important and appropriate action he or she took during the first week of the month. You have the employee's name inscribed on the plaque and wait until presentation time at your end-of-month staff meeting. The day arrives, and as you step out of your office, you see your recipient in a violent argument with a customer. The customer storms out of your building vowing never to return. Your award ceremony will be very interesting indeed.

Even without this nightmare scenario, recognition given 12 times to12 different employees in a year is far from sufficient to have an effect on company performance and morale.

Competition Error

The most detrimental part of the EOM approach to recognition is the competitive nature of the system. There is only one winner and many losers. I saw a very dramatic example of the competition error at a sales banquet where I was the speaker. Before I got up to speak, the company had the presentation of its salesperson-of-the-year awards.

The company was into recognition and reward "big time." It gave an automobile to the winner in each of several divisions. In one division, the sales manager talked for at least five minutes explaining how difficult it had been to choose the winner from the top two finalists. The winner got a new midsized Chevrolet. The man who came in second received a toy model of a Rolls Royce valued at over $100.

Even though it was a classy model—the doors opened, the lights worked, the company had even thoughtfully provided the batteries—can you imagine how the second-place salesperson felt? I seriously doubt that this employee rejoiced in the success of the winner.

Some companies have tried to solve the competition problem by having several "winners," possibly the top 10. However, as mentioned earlier, having a few more winners is not better; it's worse. It's one thing to shrug off the fact that you are not the best performer, but when you are not even in the top 10, it could be humiliating.

Any recognition system where one person's success limits another's is a bad system. Whether you have 1, 10, or 100 winners, there is a problem if even one person can't win because of competitive rules. When every company in the country is preaching teamwork, it doesn't make sense to use a recognition technique like this.

Contingency Error

Another problem with EOM is its distribution. Long ago, organizations realized that if they gave the award to the "best" performer, the same person would win every time. To solve this problem, some companies made a rule that a person could not win the EOM award more than once a year.

This, of course, means that any trace of a contingency between performance and the award is eliminated. At this point, the award becomes a "pass-around" award. In other words, what is created is another noncontingent employee benefit. If you stay employed long enough, eventually you get your turn.

Perception Error

A brokerage firm advertised in a popular business magazine that it sent its top 10 brokers for the year on an all-expense-paid trip for two to someplace warm during the winter months. The company showed a picture of Maury, one of the 10 winners. The company was certain that it was a thrill for Maury to have his picture in the magazine.

It might have been a thrill, but not necessarily. Maury may have been embarrassed by the recognition and harassed by his coworkers for having been the chosen one. I can imagine that potential clients who responded to the ad would insist on speaking only to Maury to make sure that they got the "top performer."

Create a Bigger Winners' Circle

The goal of every organization should be to have *all* winners. How can we achieve that if our recognition systems *force* us to create losers. The goal for every organization is to make employees better than the competition, not better than each other. We certainly don't want our employees slugging it out with each other to win.

Anytime you reward the first, most, best, highest, or even most improved, you have destructive potential. The alternative is to develop *criterion* systems. When you have people working to accomplish a specific outcome, success is determined by whether the person or team reached that level, target, or goal independent of what others did. In this kind of system, you discover that people will not have secrets but will share the techniques and procedures that led to their success (sounds like something akin to teamwork).

An effective recognition system meets several important criteria: (1) it allows for an unlimited number of winners, (2) the performers know what must be accomplished to earn recognition and reward, and (3) the manager's success is tied to employees' success. In other words, a manager cannot be successful when his or her employees aren't.

We fail employees when we have losers because there is not enough room in the winners' circle. If the difference between the best performer and second place is measured in tenths or hundredths of a point, you can be sure that the difference is only numerical. There is no way that such a difference would be significant enough to merit different levels of recognition. Yet I have seen situations where two decimal places in the data were necessary to determine a winner.

The goal is to have your employees perform better than the competition. If you want competition, benchmark your company against your best competitor, and rally everyone to close the gap between you and the competitor if you are behind or widen the gap if you are ahead.

Contests

I love a contest, whether at work, at home, or at play. Golf would not be as much fun if it weren't for the $2 Nassau. So why would contests be a problem at work? Primarily because of the large tangibles associated with them. When trips, television sets, and other valuable items are given to the winner or winners, some people will lie, cheat, and sabotage others to win.

A number of years ago, I did an assessment of a national sales promotion sponsored by a major U.S. corporation where the top 2,500 winners of the contest got trips to the Superbowl. From the organization's perspective, it was highly successful because of the difference between the cost of the trips and the increase in the value of new sales. However, on a closer look at the data, it was discovered that less than 20 percent of the sales force had earned significant points toward the trip. During an interview, one nonwinner was asked how many points he had earned. He answered, "Did I get any points? If I did, it was a coincidence. The day they announced the contest, I knew who would win from this office. They always do."

The contest was credited with generating $65 million in additional sales on an investment of $36 million, but just think what would have happened if the contest had been structured in a way that got the other 80 percent of the sales force to participate.

This is the problem with most contests that involve money or its equivalent as prizes. They are highly motivating to the winners and a turnoff to the losers. Remember, those "losers" also work for the company.

Contests That Motivate

To run an effective contest, there are a few rules to follow:

1. Use small, tangible items as prizes, and focus on bragging rights as the main reward.
2. Next, make the contest short, usually not longer than a quarter. Year-long contests put all the consequences too far from the behavior, and even the highest performers will tend to get weary by the end of the year.
3. Most of all make the contest fun! When there are only a few large, tangible prizes, it takes out the fun for most people.
4. Finally, make sure that everyone can win. Set equivalent criteria to be reached for all teams or individuals. Do not set a limit on the number of winners, and you will discover that you may have more winners than you ever dreamed.

Embarrassment Awards

When I say make recognition fun, that does not include the kind of contest where the winners eat steak and the losers eat beans. I have seen a wide variety of embarrassment awards such as the "Pigpen Award" for poor housekeeping and the "8-Ball Award" for the poorest performer or group of performers. These kinds of activities are very risky.

Public humiliation is at the top of most peoples' list of fears. Some people will lie, cheat, and steal to avoid embarrassment. Others will approach the workplace with cynicism and depression.

Poor performers need positive reinforcement for improvement, not punishment for trying to improve, which is what these programs do. There are better ways to have fun at work.

Suggestion Systems

Any company that has a formal suggestion system will never have full engagement of employees in the work of the organization. Have you ever thought of why a suggestion box was created in the first place? Was it that employees wanted privacy? Why? Was it because if people knew the idea, they might question whether it was the idea of the suggester? There are too many problems associated with suggestion systems to recommend them. There are problems with competition, attribution, payment, and implementation. Managers are too hooked on the reported dollars saved to look at the hidden costs associated with lower morale, low rates of employee collaboration, poor teamwork, and poor realization of the reported value of the idea.

Let's say that you have the germ of an idea that could save your company millions of dollars. Let's also say that you could earn a cash award of $50,000 if the idea is accepted. Would you bring the idea to work and ask the help of your coworkers and supervisor to iron out the details, or would you go home, get in your basement, close the blinds, and work on "your idea" in your spare time?

Not long ago, after I had made a speech on a related subject, a man told me, "I've got an idea that will save this company $250,000 this year, guaranteed! And I ain't telling nobody." He went on to tell me about some politics and rules in his company's system that would possibly keep him from getting the award. His solution was to sit on the idea until "the time was right."

Large cash awards to individuals often generate hard feelings among coworkers. I discourage it. It's much better to use a small tangible or a symbolic reward rather than large cash awards. Ideas have value only when they are implemented successfully. It usually takes many people and much effort to integrate ideas into the normal routine. The behaviors of making those ideas work need to be reinforced and rewarded.

Think also what it would be like to work in a place where there were hundreds of attempts being made and reinforced every day to make the business work better. It would indeed be a place of joy and gladness.

If you look at the suggestion rates that are reported on the Internet (the numbers are of suggestions submitted in the average suggestion system), it appears that the rate of suggestions in the United States is less than one suggestion per employee per year. Despite much work to increase the numbers, they have remained the same for almost 40 years. The numbers are consistent with an engagement rate of U.S. employees of less than 30 percent. Many executives proudly advertise rates of one idea for every employee, whereas in Japan rates of over 50 suggestions per employee per year are common.

Finding Joy and Gladness at Work

Several years ago our company visited a Fuji Electric plant just outside of Tokyo as a part of a study group. Before the meeting started, I looked

through their annual report. I saw some numbers th.
suggestion-system data, but they were so large that I was ;
reading them correctly. As the meeting started, I asked the p.
to explain the numbers. It was suggestion-system data. This
about 1,500 employees had over 193,330 ideas submitted, wi. ᴜ/ percent implemented.

An engineer from a highly respected U.S. computer manufacturer
leaned over to me and said, "I'll bet some of them weren't worth a dime!"
I'm sure he was right. Some of these suggestions weren't worth much, but
the process that encourages the generation of many suggestions is worth
millions. Unfortunately, in U.S. business, we too often believe "if it ain't
big, we're not interested."

About now you may be thinking that you are tired of hearing about
Japanese management methods, but rather than being defensive about
their success, we should examine how we can profit from what they have
learned. An element of the Fuji Electric suggestion system that I particularly liked was its theme: "Finding joy and gladness at work." This single
program provided 193,330 occasions for finding joy and gladness at that
plant in 1979. Do we have *anything* that compares with that? For comparison, a similar plant in the United States at the same time would have been
proud if they produced 1,500 suggestions annually.

The Japanese seem to have a shaping culture. They practice the saying
in Japan that "Many raindrops make an ocean." *Kaizen* (improvement) is
almost a way of life in Japan. The Japanese are much more likely to celebrate small improvements than we are. They know that somebody sub-
mitting an idea that "ain't worth a dime" today may, if reinforced, submit
one worth a million dollars tomorrow.

Group Incentives

The research has been equivocal on the effect of group pay on performance and satisfaction. It seems to be clear that group incentives improve
the performance of hourly paid employees. However, as researchers isolate
variables that affect performance under these plans, new findings are
emerging. It seems that while there may be some benefit to the organization in improved performance on the variable that is rewarded, the gain
may be more than offset by the negative effect that it has on the organization's best performers.

For example, Honeywell, Dickinson, and Poling (1997) found that when given a choice, high performers chose the individual incentive system, and low performers chose the group incentive system. London and Oldham (1977) found that low performers performed the same when paid group-based incentives and individual incentives. However, higher performers performed an average of 17 percent lower when paid group-based incentives.

Although group incentives do improve performance of hourly paid employees, they have a negative effect on the most productive performers. Average performers seem to be split in preference for group incentives. Therefore, when satisfaction scores are taken across high, average, and low performers, the numbers tend to show satisfaction with the plan, although the high performers that you most want to reward are the ones who wind up being the most dissatisfied—not a good outcome.

Annual Bonus Plans

From what we know about reinforcement, the typical end-of-the-year bonus has a limited effect on performance. The fact that people will choose small immediate rewards over larger delayed ones has been substantiated by many researchers, including Herrnstein (1990), Ainslie (1975), Davison and McCarthy (1988), and Green, Myerson, and Ostaszewski (in press). Although it is possible to have a reward so large that it will be preferred over a small one, the amount required is impractical in most situations at work. State lotteries are a current example where people will play even though the probability of winning is very, very small. The reason is that the cost to play is small and the rewards are huge—usually hundreds of millions of dollars.

I have concluded from the available research that (1) if a bonus is uncertain (meaning that there may not be funds to pay it), it has minimal effect on day-to-day performance; (2) if a bonus is certain (meaning the money will be paid if performance merits it), it has to be quite large to have substantial effect on performance; and (3) when the bonus is delayed and uncertain, the bonus is no more effective than any other form of delayed compensation.

Does this mean that bonuses should be eliminated? Not necessarily, but to make them effective, you need to have a way to measure bonus-eligible achievement on a continuous basis and have frequent feedback on progress. Combining social reinforcement for progress with a delayed and uncertain bonus can overcome some of the drawbacks associated with this form of organizational reward.

Gain Sharing

Although there are many forms of gain sharing, practically all have problems with delay, uncertainty, and control. In most of the plans, there is a formula to determine the amount to be shared and a formula to determine the distribution to employees.

The gain-sharing pool is usually determined by a formula that calculates the gains as a function of cost reduction or productivity improvements. The distribution to employees is typically based on pay, length of service, or some other nonperformance variable. The concept of gainsharing is good, but the methods of distributing the gains is usually far from ideal. The methods of determining the amount of money to be distributed are fiscally sound. The problem is with the way the individuals earn their share.

If the money is given without regard to an individual's contribution to the organizational result, you would not expect a poor or even average performer to become more productive or efficient as a result of receiving gain sharing. For gain sharing to be effective over the long run, the system must have the capability of measuring and rewarding individual contributions.

That is, the gains should be divided based on individual contributions, not by team membership or shift or other group performance. Bill Abernathy developed what he called a *profit-indexed performance pay system* that is designed based on what is known from the behavior analytical research on pay. It is detailed in his book *The Sin of Wages* (Abernathy & Associates, 1996). Let's say here that pay is distributed based on performance. There are no formulas by which economic gains are shared across the board. While it is more trouble for accounting, employees are happier, and future gains are more likely.

Too Little, Too Few, Too Late

By this point in this chapter, you should understand the relevant characteristics of positive reinforcement that are critical to the effectiveness of any organizational system that is designed to affect performance. (That is, of course, all organizational systems!) Let me summarize.

ients of positive reinforcement are (1) that the conse-
valued by the person receiving it, (2) it must be contin-
.. performance, (3) there must be some way for employees to track
the gains, at least monthly, and (4) it must be delivered frequently (more
than annually). When you understand that for recognition and rewards to
have an effect on behavior they must meet these criteria, you can begin to
understand why there are so many problems with these systems. They lack
almost all the critical characteristics. They are almost always delayed.
Because they are delayed, the link between the behavior and the reward or
recognition is weak. Because reward and recognition cost money, they
certainly are not given frequently. Finally, noncash recognition is limited
to a few items or privileges and, as such, may appeal to only a few people.
If the reward is cash, the amount available is not usually meaningful to
most employees.

Making Rewards and Recognition Effective

1. *Positive reinforcement has to be a daily affair.* No matter how much
   money or time you spend on rewards and recognition, you will not get
   the results you want, or could have, if the organization gets things done
   with negative reinforcement day to day. Think about it. How much
   money would it take to make you happy if, hour by hour, you were
   being threatened, embarrassed, confronted, and pressured? This does
   not generate excitement about work and accomplishments. As Tom
   Odom of Shell Oil said, "It's hard to celebrate when you've been beat
   up on the way to the party."

2. *The reward and recognition must be earned.* There must be a direct relationship between individual performance and the reward and recognition. One of the real problems with team recognition and rewards is
   that everyone gets them whether they contribute equally or not. This is
   not usually a problem for the poor performers, but it causes considerable heartburn for the top performers over a period of time.

3. *The recognition must have personal value.* The dollar value of the recognition is unimportant as long as the items are meaningful to the performers. If it creates a positive memory of some accomplishment, the amount
   of money spent on recognition is irrelevant. The T-shirt, coffee mug, or
   key chain will be valuable only if it is combined with, or reminds the

person of, an accomplishment that makes the performer proud. Telling people they should be proud does not make them proud.

4. *The delay between the behavior and the reward and recognition must be bridged.* Because reinforcement is immediate, some event that has reinforcing value must occur in proximity to the valued behavior or performance. Awarding points that are related to an incentive are one way to bridge the gap. The points must be paired frequently with social reinforcement to enhance motivational value.

5. *The presentation of the incentive should be preceded by a celebration.* A celebration in this context is an opportunity for the performers to relive the accomplishment. The participants, not the bosses, should be asked to recount the things they did to meet the goal. Done this way, the incentive anchors a memory of an accomplishment and, as such, is more valuable.

6. *Money is not the best incentive.* Although money can be used occasionally, it should not be the main incentive. Even though most people like money, it provides limited reinforcement for the cost. Money is soon spent, and the memory of it soon fades, whereas other tangible incentives are kept longer and act as a constant reminder of some accomplishment. If celebrated appropriately, the behaviors involved in producing the results will be remembered long after the memory of the cash has faded away.

Relationships Make It Happen

I was talking to a senior manager in her office one day when the topic turned to recognition. She said derisively, "I just got recognized with a 'black onyx pen-and-pencil set.'" She was pointing to a plastic pen-and-pencil set on her desk that was definitely not black onyx. She continued, "My boss didn't even have the decency to present it to me in person. It just appeared on my desk today."

As she talked, it became clear that she didn't have much respect for the boss. The conversation was not really about the pen-and-pencil set; it was really about her relationship with her boss. Her boss was like many others I have known. He thought that the "black onyx" pen-and-pencil set was the positive reinforcer and that he was a positively reinforcing person. As it turned out, he was the only one who thought so.

There are a great many managers in organizations today who think because they give people pay raises, promotions, and various rewards and recognition, they are effective managers who are perceived positively by the people who work for them. They are usually shocked when they find out through a morale survey or in some other way that they are not.

If people don't like you, practically nothing you do will be received well. You can brag on them, give them money and merchandise, and it will do little to change their opinion. To make reinforcement, reward, and recognition effective, you must first develop good relationships with people. Although some companies still have some onerous supervisors and managers, they are a vanishing breed. It is risky business today for companies to promote supervisors and managers on the basis of technical and professional skills while minimizing or excusing their weaknesses in social skills.

Years ago I constructed a short survey to measure the extent that managers were using positive reinforcement as a management practice. The question that accounted for the most variance was, "Do you like your supervisor?" If workers didn't like their supervisors, nothing the supervisor did in a formal way had the intended or desired effect. If they liked the supervisor, the employees would overlook some of his or her shortcomings.

How do you establish good relationships? Most people don't need to be told how to do this. As Dale Carnegie said, "Liking someone is the other side of having them like you." By this point in the book, I don't need to go into detail about how you can accomplish this, but I will say that the first order of business is to establish yourself as a positive reinforcer by taking an interest in what is important to your boss, colleagues, and other employees. Try to establish your presence as an antecedent for good things. Rather than saying something can't be done, say something like, "I will start working on it right away." Not that you will ignore poor performance, or even poor habits, but that the most interactions are positive.

Remember that just being positive will not make you a good manager because if you are positive at the wrong time, in the wrong way, or at the wrong frequency, you will surely be ineffective in your relationships. However, you surely can't be the most effective manager if you are not a positively reinforcing person.

Relationships are the foundation on which effective rewards and recognition are built. When you have that positive foundation, your opinions, needs, and interests will matter to those above and below you in the management hierarchy. It may be trite to say, but when employees know you care about them, they will care about you. Positive relationships enhance rewards and recognition. If you don't have a positive relationship with the people you work with, you will waste your time trying to create discretionary performance, and it will be a very hard job.

16

Compensation and Performance Appraisal

Compensation and performance appraisal are two of the most talked-about aspects of corporate life. Unfortunately, most of the talk is negative. Neither compensation nor appraisal, as they are usually administered, brings out the best in people.

Entire books have been written about both subjects, a number of prominent firms specialize in compensation consulting, and myriad training programs have been developed to train managers to design and conduct effective performance appraisals. So, in this one chapter, I can't even begin to describe specific prescriptions for curing the ills so many good intentions have created in these two important areas. If you are interested in more detail, see Aubrey Daniels, *OOPS! 13 Management Practices That Waste Time & Money (and what to do instead)* (Performance Management Publications, 2009) and Aubrey Daniels and Jon Bailey, *Performance Management: Changing Behavior That Drives Organizational Effectiveness*, 6th ed. (Performance Management Publications, 2014).

What I will try to do is make you aware of specific problems with traditional appraisal and compensation systems. The principles in this book and the ideas explained in this chapter should provide you with guidance to help you increase the effectiveness of these two systems in your company.

Compensation as Reward

The hope of receiving a reward (positive, future, and uncertain [PFU]) is an ineffective motivating factor for getting a response, and as has been said many times in this book, it is not sufficient to maximize performance. Rewards that are positive, future, and certain (PFC) don't exert much influence on daily behavior either. Therefore, regular compensation can't maximize performance, but it can help or hinder.

Money is important. Very few people can afford to work without being paid, but contrary to popular belief, money is not the most important consideration when people are working. The way people are treated at work every day is much more important for determining performance than the money they receive at the end of the month or year. When we work, we expect to be paid fairly and competitively for what we do. However, some compensation plans actually work against day-to-day motivation; therefore, it's important to know when this is occurring and make adjustments.

Frederick Herzberg, Bernard Mauser, and Barbara Snyderman, in their book *The Motivation to Work* (Wiley, 1959), said that pay is a "dissatisfier" which will not make workers happy at work but can be, and often is, a source of considerable dissatisfaction. The source of the dissatisfaction ultimately lies in the design of the compensation plan. Although the design of the plan is determined by things such as philosophy of pay, company resources, competitiveness, and profit margins, in the end for the employee it all comes down to "How much money do I get and how can I get more?"

Following are some of the problems with the usual compensation designs as seen from the performance management perspective.

Compensation Is a Positive, Future, and Certain (PFC)

With layoffs and termination more frequent in today's business environment, some might consider compensation as a PFU, but for the person who is working, it is a PFC. However, the time lag between the behavior and the receipt of compensation poses an obvious performance problem. Most employees don't consider salary or even weekly pay when working day to day. When employees are performing with an eye toward a regular weekly, biweekly, or monthly paycheck, other more *immediate consequences* are likely to pull them off track. We all have had those days when we started out to accomplish something and spent the whole day working only to find at the end of the day that we had not done anything that was the priority at the beginning of the workday. To minimize these distractions, I recommend moving reinforcement (nonfnancial) as close to performance (priority) as possible. Whenever I have been able to position consequences, particularly positive reinforcement, closer to behavior, I have never failed to increase performance, even with people paid by piecework or commission. When performance increased, the performers' compensation also increased, but it was made possible by positive, immediate consequences.

Regular paydays don't influence daily behavior, but even less effective are the usual attempts companies make to motivate performance improvement using money. *Annual bonuses*, a typical attempt at associating improved performance with increased compensation, are almost always a PFU. As such, bonuses have little daily motivational value. These plans usually turn out to be an increased expense to the company rather than an investment that pays performance dividends.

The same can be said for the typical *profit-sharing* plan. Profit-sharing plans provide as uncertain a consequence as you can find. The reason that profit-sharing plans can't improve performance is that profits are out of the average performer's control in most jobs. An employee can work as hard as he or she can, and there may be no profit. The Internal Revenue Service (IRS), accounting and executive decisions, and even the exchange rate of the dollar can, in some companies, have much more bearing on profit than the performer's work.

Remember from previous chapters that people should not be rewarded or punished for results that are out of their control. When profits are available and are shared, employees like it; when profits are too small to share, employees are disappointed. In either case, the reward is too far removed from employee behavior to influence performers to do anything different. While people like bonuses, that doesn't consistently translate into better performance.

Pay and Contingency

The most serious problem in the typical compensation plan is the lack of performance contingencies. As you know, every performer has choices about how well to perform the tasks that make up a job.

With the usual salary and wage systems, whether you work hard today or you don't will make no difference in your next paycheck. Whether you take a little extra time to make sure that things are done correctly or do or make impulsive decisions and do little follow-up, you will still get your paycheck, and it will be for the same amount. Traditional compensation plans have very little impact on behavioral contingencies that affect daily performance.

Pay as a Form of Competition

Most pay raises are competitive. Because there is a finite amount of money to be divided among employees, if one person gets more than the average raise, someone will get less than the average. In other words, one person's financial gain is another person's financial loss.

Because most organizations have not developed an accurate method for appraising performance, the decisions about average versus above average are frequently debated and the final decision may have deleterious effects on teamwork and cooperation. The way most companies minimize competition for compensation is to give everyone an across-the-board increase. Of course, this exacerbates the problem of *equal treatment of unequals*, and I've already written about how demotivating this practice can be. As mentioned earlier, the only people who are unhappy with this tactic are your best performers.

Noncontingent Benefits

Other than attracting good people, all the average company gets from the typical company benefit plan is a higher cost of doing business. It is rare that there is any performance contingency tied to increases in benefits. Unfortunately, in some companies, executives expect increases in motivation and performance as a result of improvements in benefits. They shouldn't count on it.

While attractive benefits help companies to recruit good people, a good benefit plan will not increase motivation and performance unless performance contingencies are associated with the plan. Even the popular "cafeteria" plans don't affect employee performance. People do like them, but again, the poor performers get to choose just as freely as the outstanding performers. If your company chooses to increase benefits, I have no problem if it is happy with what it gets. While they may score points in the "Best Places to Work" survey, benefits don't necessarily get high performance.

Performance Appraisal

Over the years, my consultants and I have seen the performance-appraisal programs of hundreds of companies. And I have finally come to this conclusion: *apart from documentation for legal purposes, the annual performance appraisal is a waste of time.* See *OOPS! 13 Management Practices That Waste Time & Money (and what to do instead)* (Performance Management Publications, 2009) for a detailed explanation.

The managers who do the appraisals don't like them, nor do the performers receiving them. It is a masochistic and sadistic ritual of business. The way we appraise employees must change.

Employees are usually appraised on some form of rating scale. Three-point, five-point, seven-point, sometimes 10-point scales are used. In any case, *the highest number on the scale usually represents outstanding performance, and the lowest number on the scale*, 1 or 0, represents poor performance. Each employee must fall somewhere on the scale.

A number of techniques may be used to come up with this final rating. One that is particularly bad, but very popular, is to rate the employee on a number of performance factors on the same scale, add all the numbers, and divide by the number of factors considered. This usually gives you a whole number and a fraction (3.17, for example), which you then round off to the nearest whole number. That number is the employee's rating.

In a typical measurement system, there is no way that the differences between the scores represent real differences in performance, with the possible exception of comparing employees who are at the extremes, for example, comparing those who are at the ends of the distribution—the best with the worst. We treat differences as real, however, because the ratings carry real consequences with them. However, the differences have real financial and social consequences.

If you give mediocre performance ratings to a high performer, you will eventually make that person a mediocre performer. If you give high performance ratings to a mediocre performer, you will continue to have a mediocre performer.

Some organizations have tried to make performance appraisals more effective by rating performance more often. They now do semiannual or quarterly ratings. These companies keep people stirred up constantly. I have somewhat facetiously told managers how to double the effectiveness of their performance appraisal system: *do the appraisals half as often*. If the system is flawed, doing it more often is not better, it is worse!

Some human relations experts have suggested that the problem with the appraisal process is that financial consequences and the appraisal are closely associated, so they separate the two discussions. This just creates more paperwork for managers and supervisors and adds to the frustration of employees. I have not met anyone in business who thinks that there is no connection between their appraisal rating and their pay. The reason they are separated is to try to make a bad system better. It doesn't. At most, it makes the appraisal session with the employee easier for the appraiser.

Forced Ranking—As Bad As It Gets

As bad as the appraisal process may sound so far, forced ranking makes it worse because it puts limits on the number of employees who can fall into each rating group. This is known as a *forced ranking or forced distribution system*. It surprises me that there are still book writers and bloggers who recommend force ranking. They apparently follow Jack Welch's original advice (at General Electric) that because most managers and supervisors will not make the tough decision relative to accurately appraising performance, particularly giving poor ratings, the system must force such decisions and discussions.

Many managers think that they don't have a forced ranking system when, in reality, they do. The acid test of whether you have a forced ranking system is this: can every performer get the highest ranking at the same time? If they can't, then you have a forced ranking system. For example, let's say that you are responsible for the appraisal of 20 people. Let's also say that your rating system uses a five-point scale, where a rating of 1 is "poor" and a 5 is "outstanding."

After you have completed rating all 20 employees, go to your boss and say, "Boss, you're gonna' love this. All 20 of my staff got 5s." If your boss says anything other than "Great!" you have a forced ranking system.

The system that most companies use forces performers into a distribution that is some variation of the normal curve. Figure 16-1 illustrates a typical distribution.

Using this curve, you are "forcing" roughly 70 percent of the performers to be average or below average. What organization can survive in

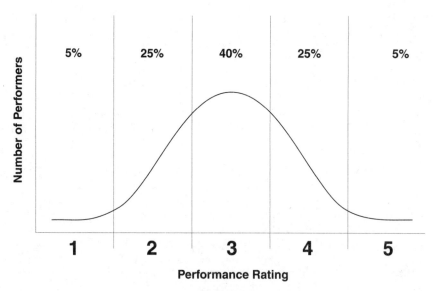

Figure 16-1 Normal curve: Performance rating distribution.

today's economy with only 30 percent of its employees above average? (It is interesting that this is about the same distribution of engaged employees.) In reality, most organizations have a distribution that is skewed to the right, allowing more employees to be rated above average. In any event, this is not a true picture of performance but an attempt to minimize complaints and maintain morale. See Figure 16-2.

A forced distribution of any kind creates unhealthy competition among employees. One employee's high rating "forces" someone else to get a lower rating because only one employee can occupy each spot on the curve. Employees who continue to try to get the top rating and end up in the next-to-the-highest group eventually quit trying (extinction).

Proponents of this system say that if you measure people on almost any variable, you will get a normal distribution. In other words, performance is probably normally distributed, so forced ranking should be fair. The problem with this logic is that organizations don't hire on the basis of a normal distribution. No executive has ever complained that we don't have enough below average employees.

Every organization I know hires as many people as it can who are in the 90th percentile or better of whatever selection indicators are used. However, after such organizations have gone to the trouble of hiring the

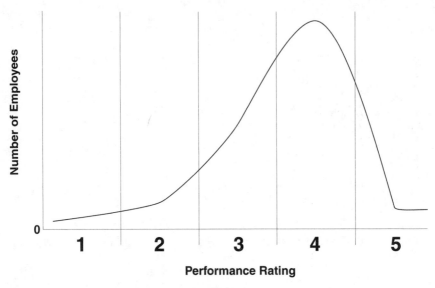

Figure 16-2 Typical performance rating distribution.

best people available, they force them into the normal appraisal distribution, and some of them will be labeled "average." In an engineering company where I worked, it was an unwritten rule that no new employee could receive more than an average rating because that employee would be competing against experienced engineers—the thought being that it is better to upset a new employee than a veteran.

The forced ranking system certainly makes the distribution of raises and bonuses easier for managers and supervisors. Finance loves it because compensation costs are easier to control, but to pretend that it truly evaluates worker performance is a sham.

Pinpointing Results: The Performance Matrix

The first thing to do to improve the effectiveness of compensation and appraisal systems is to pinpoint the results and behaviors needed from every job. If you recall, this is the first step in performance management.

By having specific results and behaviors for which you are accountable, it is easy to see how you as the performer are doing each day. The best job you will ever have is one where you know how you performed at the end of every day. By the way, most athletes have this kind of job.

Could that be a factor in why many people love sports as a hobby and as a career?

By planning how much you need to do each day, you have a performance appraisal that can be done every day. It is certainly not practical for management to measure performance every day, even if measures are available. However, if performance can be monitored by the performer, it is possible to get the benefits of daily measurement without the high cost of management time. At Morningside Academy, every student gets a report card every day! It has to be a large factor in the high rate of learning at the school. Not only does the student see what he or she accomplished and what needs more work, but the teacher is also able to see what the student accomplished relative to what was planned. It doesn't hurt that the parents also know.

An ideal format for this is the *performance matrix*. The performance matrix allows us to measure every job, from the boardroom to the shop floor. The matrix is ideal because it is totally flexible and makes it possible to customize it for every person and change it as business or job responsibilities change. If someone is on a production job one month and is changed to a creative job the next month, performance can be exemplary in both jobs. The performance matrix lets you measure how well the performer is doing against expectations regardless of job.

Figure 16-3 is an example of a completed performance matrix. A score of 5 is the baseline performance. A score of 10 indicates goal performance. Scores from 11 to 13 are overachievement. Scores on the various performances can be anchored by counts, checklists, or behaviorally anchored rating scales.[1]

Anchors and their values can be changed as often as conditions change, but I recommend that you not change more often than monthly. If a new process is introduced on the job, you can very easily change the scores, the weights, and their corresponding anchors. As priorities change, the weightings of the various items on the matrix also can be changed. The weighting represents the percent of time that a person is expected to spend on any particular result or behavior. Although weighting is rather difficult to do in the beginning, it is of considerable value to the performer and the boss. Practice and adjustments during early attempts will improve your skills in determining weighting.

From an organizational perspective, the ability to shift weightings allows the company to rapidly shift the value of performance to meet the

Name __A. Daniels__ Position _____ Manager _____ Date __02/1/16__

BEHAVIORS/RESULTS

PINPOINTS	4	5	6	7	8	9	10	11	12	13	x WEIGHT	POINTS
Employee Contacts (Non-office)	<2	2	4	6	8	10	12	15	20	(25+)	15	195
Improve PM Seminar (Documented Changes)	<2	2	4		(6)		10	To Tracy 11/11	By 11/7	By 11/4	10	80
Complete EOM Article		Review Billie's input		Add research		Revised draft	Final draft	Before Thanks-giving	By 11/14		15	165
Review Direct Reports' Matrices	<2		2	3	4	5	6	50% in person	75%	100%	20	220
Commitments Met (Percent on time)	<75%	Record		90%	(95%)		100%	Early			15	120
Customer Contact (from Checklist)	<3				4	6	8	12	(16)	20	15	180
Administrative (See Checklist)	<6	6	7	8	9	10	(11)	+3	+6	+10	10	100

SCORE __1060__

REINFORCEMENT PLAN

Points	R+	Comments	Plans
1000	Golf	No score below 8	Friday afternoon
1200	Golf	No score below 10	Friday A.M. golf

Next Review Date __05/1/16__

1993–2016 Aubrey Daniels International

Figure 16-3 Performance matrix.

changing needs of internal and external customers as well as changes in the work unit itself. An item that may have had a 10-point value one month may have a 30-point value the next month because of a customer emergency. Because of a shift to a new process, cost may be minimized, whereas yield may be more important. These shifts can be easily accommodated on the matrix by changing the weightings of those items.

With this type of system, you have a foundation for both appraisal and compensation systems. This matrix system allows you to accurately tie future pay and other recognition and rewards to day-to-day performance.

Appraisals and Contingent Compensation

With a performance matrix, you can predetermine performance targets and their consequences, financial and social. Consistent scores above 1,000 might result in a preferred assignment, a bonus, or a raise in pay.

Under this system, an organization would want all performers to get the maximum rating because high ratings would result in high value to the organization. The matrix connects employee success to organizational success. The manager who has developed a good performance matrix is ensuring that both the performer and the organization are getting their money's worth. The matrix method eliminates peer competition because every performer is competing against his or her own targets and goals. It permits a supervisor to tailor each person's performance and development plan to the needs of the performer and the organization without regard to what others are doing.

Compensation and the Matrix

Once you have the matrix in place, you can have a true pay-for-performance system. Dollars can be tied to matrix scores, which should be tied to value-added behaviors and results.

In setting up the matrix, all aspects of effective reinforcement and reward can be taken into account. Obviously, items on the matrix must be within the control of the performer, but when they are, contingency is built into the process (i.e., you earn a score, you get the consequences stated).

The reinforcement plan associated with the matrix allows you to tailor the plan to the individual. Because the supervisor, coach, or team leader knows the results for which performers are accountable and the behaviors and accomplishments that are associated with them, he or she will be able to reinforce immediately and frequently. Because performers are also aware of these expectations, they are potentially able to provide self-reinforcement as well. Every time the performers engage in the desired behaviors or make progress toward the final goal, they can see their progress and reinforce themselves.

Increasing Bonus and Gain-Sharing Plan Effectiveness

The effectiveness of bonus and gain-sharing programs can be increased considerably by the matrix. Take a typical gain-sharing program. Let's say that there are 50 employees in the plan. Let's also say that there is $50,000 in the pool and that it will be shared equally. This means that each employee would get $1,000. This method of distribution rewards poor performers and good performers equally. You know by now that this is a problem.

Using a matrix, a better distribution system could be developed. Under this system, each person would have the *opportunity* to earn an equal share *depending on performance*. Using the preceding example, if one of the 50 people scored 800 on the matrix, he might get $800 of the $1,000 available. If another scored 1,000 points, she would get the full $1,000. Those who achieved over 1,000 points may be eligible for additional recognition and rewards—usually noncash such as an afternoon or day off with pay.

If the performance of the group as a whole does not merit distribution of the budgeted amount of the pool, the remainder should not be given out. In other words, if $2,000 is left over after all earned monies are distributed, do not redistribute it among the highest performers because redistributing the excess among the best performers allows them to benefit from the poor performance of their peers and could introduce unhealthy competition again.

How About Equity?

Equity in rewards is the responsibility of the supervisor and should be an item on the supervisor's matrix. The supervisor and his or her boss should discuss what is involved in the tasks that are on the matrix so that there is *perceived* as well as *real* equity.

If you get complaints about equity, you should check them out. However, if you reinforce complaining, you will get more of it. For example, if you ask someone to do something, and that person asks, "What am I going to get for it?" you know that you have been reinforcing the wrong behavior. If someone complains about what someone else is getting and you reinforce it, you are teaching people to be jealous.

When one employee complains about what another employee is getting, your first response should be, "Do you want what that person is getting?" It might surprise you that many times the person does not want what the other person has but just wants to complain about it. If you reinforce this kind of behavior, you will create petty jealousies among performers.

However, if the employee says, "Yes, I want what he's got," then say, "Good. Let's talk about how you can earn it." In many cases, when the behaviors and performance are pinpointed for the complainer, he decides that he doesn't want the reward at that price. If he still wants it, you have an additional way to reinforce and reward improved performance.

Taking Action

I recognize that most managers reading this book will not have sufficient flexibility where pay and benefits are concerned to implement a fully contingent compensation plan. In fact, the bulk of this book is dedicated to bringing out the best in people *in spite of traditional compensation and appraisal systems*. However, there is nothing to prevent you from using a matrix system without financial rewards.

If you can affect the way your organization handles these two vital systems, I urge you to consider how you can apply these basic performance management techniques. Compensation and performance appraisal systems are for the most part well intended, but as my mama used to say, "Good intentions pave the road to hell!

Notes

1. For a detailed description, see Aubrey Daniels and Jon Bailey, *Performance Management: Changing Behavior That Drives Organizational Effectiveness*, 6th ed. (Peachtree, GA: Performance Management Publications, 2014).

17

Employee Engagement

It's Not About the Employees

If you have read this far, you know that this whole book is about engagement. The concept of discretionary effort is about how to cause employees to want to give their best every day. This chapter will attempt to compare the performance management technology to other methods being sold today as ways to attain an engaged workforce—methods that I consider incomplete, wrong, or both.

In a commercial for Fiber One cereal, a woman pulls up by a Fiber One truck at a stoplight. She rolls down the window and yells to the driver, "I just love your cereal, there. It's got such high flavor. There's no way it is just 80 calories! Right? No way. Right?

The driver responds, "Lady, I just drive the truck."

She continues, "There is no way! Right? Right?"

The driver, ignoring her question, says as he drives away, "Have a nice day."

This reminds me of a story Paul Broyhill, of Broyhill Furniture, tells about himself as a young man working at the furniture company his father owned. One day one of their largest customers was in town and wanted to play golf, but Paul's father was busy and asked Paul to play golf with the customer. As they were playing, Paul noticed that the customer was not recording his score accurately. After several instances of telling Paul an

incorrect score, Paul questioned him, saying that he must have miscounted, and as he was recalling the shots, the customer shouted, "Are you accusing me of cheating?" and got in the golf cart and drove off.
Paul walked back and reluctantly went to his father's office. His father said to Paul, "Let me explain something to you, son. You thought you were playing golf, but you were supposed to be selling furniture."

The driver in the Fiber Once commercial thought he was just driving a cereal truck when company executives also wanted him to be selling cereal. The driver in the commercial was not fully engaged in the business of Fiber One.

Jack Gordon, of Rubbermaid, was visiting a trucking company that had installed the performance management process when on one of the loading docks a forklift driver with a load of Rubbermaid merchandise stopped for Jack and his escort to pass. As Jack walked by, he noticed that the load was Rubbermaid products. He said to the forklift driver, "Be careful with that load, son. I work for Rubbermaid."

Without missing a beat, the driver replied, "I do too, sir." This forklift driver appeared to be fully engaged in his work the way the trucking company wanted him to be.

Wouldn't it be great if all employees responded this way? Well, they don't. In fact, according to a Gallop survey, less than one-third of employees say they are fully engaged.[1] What this means is that only one of three employees who see something that needs to be done but that is not explicitly in their job description actually does it. Because this is by the employees' own admission, I suspect that the numbers are actually lower because there are likely some employees who are not engaged but do not want to admit that on a survey. Not only are the employee engagement numbers low, but they have been low for as long as they have been studied (1990s).

I don't understand why, considering numbers like these, executives would not declare "corporate war" on disengagement. The amount of money "left on the table" as a result of this disengagement is significant. The organizational benefits for high economic returns produced by engaged employees are probably better than that of any other initiative a corporation can undertake. No matter what the initiative is, its success and the ability to sustain the gains are almost totally dependent on what people do and how they do it.

To get an idea of what is at stake here, Thomas Gilbert, author of *Human Competence: Engineering Worthy Performance* (Pfeiffer, 2009),

$$PIP = \frac{Wex}{Wt}$$

Figure 17-1   Performance improvement potential (PIP).

developed a formula to measure the economic value of bringing out the best in people. He called it a *measure of competence*, and the formula shown in Figure 17-1 measures the *performance improvement potential* (PIP) in any job.

This formula enables the PIP of *current* employees to be calculated. Simply take the best performer's production data, the *exemplar*, as Gilbert called her W_{ex}, and divide that number by W_t, the typical or average performer's production data, to get the PIP. For example, if the best performer W_{ex}, makes 120 widgets an hour and the average is 90 W_t, the PIP 120 divided by 90 would yield 1.33, or a potential improvement of 33 percent.

When you convert these numbers to dollars, the economic value of moving every performer to the exemplar level is staggering. Of course, the skeptic will say that every employee can't perform at the highest or exemplar performer level (I don't believe that, by the way), but putting that argument aside , if you calculate the value of moving everyone, every shift, every team to the current *average* level, you will also be surprised by that economic benefit. Typically, the outcome is not a small number.

Another benefit of doing this is that the improvement is available for little cost because you are already paying for it but people are not being properly motivated to do their best. The distribution division of a major retailer was able to delay plans for constructing a new multi-million-dollar center because of increased throughput of existing centers. The increases occurred not by adding employees but by increasing output per employee.

The engagement goal should be to have 100 percent of employees delivering discretionary effort every day (fully engaged). And remember, the only way to accomplish this is through positive reinforcement. You cannot *make* people give you their best. Discretionary effort is given freely.

With all the work that has been done on various ways to create cultures of engagement over the last 20 years, why have the numbers not moved appreciably? Could it be that the current approaches to addressing the problem—and there are many—are missing the mark? In my opinion, the answer is "Yes." One of the answers lies in the fact that the engagement data reveal that only one-third of managers are fully engaged. (Remember, this is by their own admission.)

I have often had executives ask, "Why don't employees act like owners?" The answer is pretty simple. They aren't owners. The more modern question is, "Why aren't more employees engaged?" My answer is, "What is it about the workplace that would cause employees to want to get engaged?" We get engaged to people, not organizations. And there is the rub. If your manager is not engaged, why would a frontline employee want to be?

A not infrequent statement in many companies where employees respond to a supervisor after he has made a request of them is, "I will do this for you, but I am not doing it for the company." While at some level "the company" doesn't care what the employee says as long as the task gets done, I think everyone who has read this book to this point realizes that to have such a response from an employee is an indictment of company management rather than the employee.

One should ask how the employee developed such as attitude. Did he feel this way about the company from day one? If no, then what happened to cause him to feel as he does now? Obviously, some things have happened that the employee did not like. If employees are not engaged, it is a leadership problem. Nothing more, nothing less! Level of engagement is a reflection of the aggregate of management behaviors, decisions, policies, and procedures.

Current engagement approaches are typified in a free e-book produced by David Zinger entitled *The Keys of Employee Engagement*. In this e-book, 12 contributors present 26 keys (A–Z) with little overlap. They present over 300 ideas, and it is clear that they just made them up. By that I mean that they were not scientifically derived but came from the contributors' experiences. I believe that we must move beyond personal experience to scientifically validated practices that work everywhere. Zinger describes many benefits to employees for being fully engaged in work, but the only problem is that they are all positive, future, and uncertain (PFU). This means that those who are not engaged are not likely to become engaged when the only consequences are PFU.

In addition, many articles and books about engagement suggest, outright or indirectly, that frontline employees have a responsibility to be engaged and help others to do the same. This is akin to saying that citizens in a country such as North Korea have a responsibility to make the government successful. Create a poor work environment, and employees will respond poorly. Create a proper workplace, and people will respond properly. Managers cannot share the responsibility for lack of engagement with employees. The relative lack of engagement is a reflection of the way people are treated by the environment managers create.

In the book *Measure of a Leader* (McGraw-Hill, 2007), my coauthor and I state, "The measure of a leader is the behavior of the followers." Without major change at the leadership level of an organization, it is akin to the saying made popular by Sara Palin, former vice presidential candidate, "like putting lipstick on a pig": the lipstick eventually wears off, and the pig is as ugly as before. A significant number of organizations have been using a lot of lipstick. Major surgery on how the organization treats people will be required for substantial and lasting improvement.

Contrary to popular opinion, the workplace creates a lack of engagement. It is not about attitude, communication, commitment, or flow. It is not about the employees at all. They can't fix it. While some employees seem to be unaffected by the way business is conducted, even they can eventually be worn down to the point that they give little or no discretionary effort—doing their job and little more.

In order to have a more practical and effective solution to the problem of employee engagement (EE), I recommend changing from EE to ER— not emergency room but *employee reinforcement*. Engagement is about how to get people to willingly do everything in their power to move the organization forward at a rapid pace. There is only one way to do this. It is with positive reinforcement. Research confirms this fact, proven with literally hundreds of studies. While the average manager understands at a commonsense level that positive reinforcement is important, positive reinforcement is not well integrated into policies, procedures, and management behaviors. Reinforce at the wrong time, for the wrong behavior, in the wrong way, and at the wrong frequency, and you get not an energized, engaged employee but just the opposite.

Years ago, when I was training supervisors to lead employee teams, I told them that a good way to get a positive response from team members is to start the first meeting by asking the group for help in solving a work-related problem. In one of the first meetings, the supervisor gave the employees a problem that engineers, locally and corporate, had failed to solve. Quality consultants were hired, and they, too, had failed. The problem occurred intermittently, and despite hundreds of thousands of dollars spent over 18 months, it had not been solved. At the first team meeting, the supervisor told employees that he had a problem and needed their help to solve it. After he explained the problem, he asked if anyone had an idea about what was causing it. A team member spoke up immediately saying, "I know what that is." It turned out that he did in fact know.

As I tell this story in some of my presentations, I ask the group, if the manager were to ask the employee, "Why didn't you tell somebody?" what do you think the employee would have said? The students almost unanimously say, "Nobody ever asked me." I have asked many groups this question for many years, and they always come up with the same answer: "Nobody asked me." I recently asked a technician for our coffee service why a certain problem seemed to occur frequently. His answer, "I know how it can be fixed, but *nobody ever asks me.*" I am not saying that frontline employees have all the answers, although they may think they do, but they will never learn if they are not allowed to give input and find out if their suggestions do or do not work.

You might say that you have a suggestion system and employees have always been encouraged to make them, and because you get suggestions, you think the system works. When I wrote the first edition of this book, American employees produced two-tenths of a suggestion a year in formal suggestion systems. (I have joked that at that time it took five Americans to have an idea.) In Fuji Electric—the Tokyo plant I visited in 1981—there were 127 suggestions per employee per year, with over 85 percent implemented. Compared to the U.S. number of 0.2 per employee per year, the Fuji employees produced 635 times more ideas per employee than Americans. While this number is almost unbelievable, we might be surprised at what would happen if we simply began to ask a very simple question of frontline employees like "What do you think we should do?"

A new general manager of a mine I worked in gathered employees together on his first day and asked what changes were needed to make the mine safer. Although it took a while to get the first item, the suggestions soon began to flow because the general manager had the head of maintenance at the table with him, and when the first item was put forth, the general manager turned to the director of maintenance and asked, "Can you fix that today?"

The maintenance manager said, "We can *start* on it today."

"Is there someone you can call and get started before this meeting is over?" the general manager asked. After he did that, the suggestions continued for over an hour. After the meeting, items that could not be fixed that day and those that needed corporate approval were posted on a chart on the general manager's door and updated weekly so that employees could track the status.

When employees have a stake in the way things are done, they become fully engaged. If my idea is used, I have an interest in the outcome and will do my best to make it successful. When you ask employees for help, they are eager to help, particularly if they know that their input will be used or at least seriously considered. Engagement is not difficult. Just asking for input can change a person's interest and actions about work.

As the general manager was leaving, after the meeting just mentioned, he asked a senior manager what he thought of the meeting. The senior manager replied, "Jim, I have always wanted to work in a plant like that, and now I do!" When employees' ideas are listened to and when some are implemented, people become more engaged. How hard is that? How much does that cost? Whose permission do you need to ask employees for their help, ideas, or opinions? Apparently by the poor results for many years, some people are making this engagement thing into something that is difficult.

Many companies have given stock and stock options to make sure that employees are engaged. As you might imagine, stock and stock options are nice, but they don't make much of a difference to employees after the day they are told about the award. As such, stock options don't engage an individual day to day. Certainly all supervisors can ask for input not only on all problems but also on how to accomplish targets such as production, quality, safety, and costs. However, in the most engaged organizations, all ideas about the physical workplace, processes, systems, and work rules should be opportunities for input from the people who actually have to work in that environment and have to implement those processes, systems, and rules. Most of the time, employees are told what they have to do rather than how they should do it.

Every president featured on *Undercover Boss* always gets valuable input from the employees about things that would make the company better. Many times the "bosses" are stunned at how poorly company policies, rules, and processes are followed. They are also embarrassed at the negative impact their executive decisions have on the frontline level. Their ideas range from pay to security and personnel. Although it is a positive event that CEOs are willing to disguise themselves and attempt frontline jobs, it is a negative that they feel they have to do so to find out what employees really feel.

If you want to become a more positively reinforcing supervisor or manager tomorrow, you can start by saying the following many times per week: "I have a problem, and I need your help." Most employees, when hearing this, will try to help you. They may not always be able to give you the help you need, but you will probably be surprised at how many times they will. In addition, when they can't help, you will have an opportunity to teach them something about the business. Every time your boss asks you to improve some aspect of the business, be it budget, costs, production, quality, or safety, ask your employees for help. "We have to cut the budget. Can you help me?" When you are asked to implement anything, ask your employees for their help before implementing. You will be surprised at how smart they are and how engaged they become in the business.

A number of years ago, I took a group of CEOs to visit a trucking company that had created an outstanding engaged workforce. Everywhere there were examples of where employees went considerably beyond what would be normally expected. One driver went home to get his personal pickup to deliver freight because his large trailer truck couldn't negotiate the snowy, icy roads that day. He had to make many trips to reload his pickup before all the freight was delivered. As the presidents were touring the shops, the shop manager was showing the CEOs a piece of equipment that one of the mechanics suggested would help improve the time it would take to rebuild engines. As Floyd, the shop manager, related the story, he said that when he heard about the piece of equipment, he presented a purchase request to his boss. His boss told him to do a return-on-investment (ROI) analysis on it. Floyd said proudly as he patted the machine, "They taught us to do an ROI, and here it is." One of the CEOs said, "What does your purchasing department think of that?" Floyd took a deep breath, grew about two inches, and replied, "Sir, you are looking at the purchasing department." That kind of engagement doesn't just happen; it was a reflection of the culture that management created by design.

I hope you recognize by now that this book is really a manual for how to get total engagement. By implementing the principles and procedures presented here, you will be able to capture discretionary effort. Not only will you see large changes in organization or unit economic outcomes, but you will also make it a great place to work.

Notes

1. Amy Adkins, "Majority of U.S. Employees Not Engaged Despite Gains in 2014," *Gallop Employee Engagement Survey*, January 28, 2015.

18

Technology and Behavior

The factory of the future will have only two employees, a man and a dog. The man will be there to feed the dog. The dog will be there to keep the man from touching the equipment.

—WARREN BENNIS, ORGANIZATIONAL CONSULTANT AND AUTHOR

Of course the challenge to management is how to get the man to consistently feed the dog.

Whether or not this scene comes to pass, technology is already changing every part of our lives. As far back as the early 1980s, Fuji Fanuc operated a factory in Japan using practically all robotics. At the end of the day shift, managers turned off the lights and went home, leaving the robots running all night to make more robots!

Today, 3D printers can print dimensional replicas of everything from a human heart to a house. Medical technology exists such that you can have a brain tumor removed and drive yourself home from the hospital the same day.[1] The amazing fact is that the rate of invention in every part of life is only getting faster. Technological changes that will occur in the next 10 to 15 years are impossible to predict.

Casey Stengel, longtime manager of the New York Yankees, said, "Never make predictions, especially about the future." Modern technology has made him seem prescient. However, one thing is easy to predict: technology will change behavior, and behavior will change technology. At this point, however, behavior and technology seem to be on different trajectories, each going it alone and intersecting only when problems arise. In this chapter you will learn why it is to everyone's advantage to integrate both behavior and technology at the point of design.

Acceptance of Technology in Business

Throughout the last century, if any change was suggested in business, particularly in manufacturing, the typical response was, "That won't work here." Why? "Cause we've never done it that way." In the mid-1970s, I worked in a textile mill that was making the same cloth on the same looms that had been used to make uniforms during the Civil War. The only difference was that looms were now powered by electricity, whereas in the 1860s they were powered by water. Change came slowly in those days,

Even today, people typically are slow to accept technological advances, particularly when technology is viewed as a threat to jobs. The Luddites in the 1700s and 1800s destroyed equipment in plants where employees saw the equipment replacing the need for their labor.

However, it is more difficult to resist technology today because it has invaded every part of our lives. We expect that every year there will be a new model of our car and that in three years or sooner our computer will be obsolete. New phones hit the market almost every year. The rate of improvement in existing products and the introduction of new products are too rapid to keep up with them.

Reluctance to accept new technology has not disappeared. Airplanes have been able to fly without a pilot for many years, but customers don't like the thought of not having a pilot in the cockpit. Technological advances typically take time for the public to adjust to them. I remember when the telephone answering machine became widely available, and the response of many people was, "Who would ever need an answering machine?" Today we accept it as a necessity. Technology changes behavior, and ultimately behavior changes technology as problems that people have with the technology lead to modification of the software and hardware.

Because developers typically don't know the science of behavior, behavior is only dealt with after a problem arises. Texting while driving is the classic example. If technology developers had some understanding of the positive reinforcement (positive, immediate, and certain consequences [PICs]) produced by using a cell phone, they would have, no doubt, been able to make a device that would have prevented texting from the driver's seat. Many apps have been developed to respond to the dangerous behavior of texting while driving only after it became evident that there was a problem. But by that time, cell phone users had already experienced the natural reinforcers built into its use. Changes after the fact that restricted use while driving would be resisted by users. Of course, as one would expect, some states are resorting to fining drivers who are texting while driving, but the fine for any particular driver will be negative, future, and uncertain (NFU) and will be no more effective than fines for speeding.

Cell phones are not the only example of how technology creates problems. In 2009, Air France Flight 447 crashed in the Atlantic Ocean killing 228 people. The plane was an Airbus that had the most technologically sophisticated cockpit instrumentation available at the time. Following the crash, a headline read, "Hi-Tech Controls Partly Blamed for Airbus Crash." A final report issued in July 2012 concluded that the accident was caused, in part, by "pilot misunderstanding of the situation leading to a lack of control of inputs *that would have made it possible to recover from it*" (italics added).

A report in 2015 by the Department of Homeland Security revealed that when screeners at airports were tested in their ability to detect banned items, they failed in 67 of 70 tests. This is a failure rate of 96 percent. However, I am doubtful that the Transportation Security Administration (TSA) knows how to solve this problem.

The problem behavior for the TSA is that because the number of bags screened each day is high, the relative presence of banned items is actually low. It is quite possible that a screener could work for many days or months and never see a banned item. This causes extinction of the correct "looking" behavior. I would suggest that knowledge about how to deal with extinction on the job does not reside in the TSA even though there are known solutions to this serious behavior problem.

The initial action by the government, that is, firing those in charge, indicates that the TSA perceives it to be a performer problem. Such actions will not solve the problem but will result in delays in applying effective solutions because it is not a personnel problem. It is a training and technology problem. How screeners are trained contributes more to finding banned items than the personal characteristics of the screeners, such as motivation and IQ. Proper training requires technology, as will be explained later, and knowledge of behavior. When behavior and technology are not integrated, significant problems occur.

Surprisingly, some companies are still slow to foresee the changes that are coming and the rate at which technology is advancing. Alan Murray, editor of *Fortune* magazine, in a report on the 2015 World Economic Forum, quoted Klaus Schwab: "The speed of innovation in terms of its development and diffusion is faster than ever." Murray concludes, "While innovation may be accelerating, most organizations aren't keeping up." Murray also states that "the ability of human systems to deal with the revolution appears to be seriously challenged."

Ray Kurzweil, American author, computer scientist, and futurist, predicts that in the next 10 years or so, over 200 of the Fortune 500 will have disappeared. A study at the John M. Olin School of Business at Washington University gives similar numbers.

In the next 10 to 15 years, the agricultural, mining, forestry, and transportation industries will employ very few people. Driverless cars and trucks will soon disrupt the transportation sector of the economy. All these changes and more indicate that companies slow to transition to new technology will be overtaken by new players.

The period of transition in the workplace from old to new technology is typically longer than it is in the consumer marketplace. While technology provides a future benefit to the owners and executives, decisions to spend money on it are typically delayed by those who are responsible for evaluating risk and returns on investment. The main reason is that in the workplace, the economic benefits of technology are often slower to be realized, whereas new technology often produces many benefits (PICs) to the consumer.

In addition, some companies move slowly to adopt new technology because their employees have been comfortably performing a job for many years, and new technology almost always upsets that comfort. Employees must be trained to use new technology, which often is anxiety provoking because it increases employees' fears that they will not be able to learn new skills and habits. New technology also raises questions about job security because more and more jobs are being replaced by technology.

The Robots Are Coming! The Robots Are Coming!

Don't worry, however, because robots will be used initially as assistants and will do most of the jobs that people don't like to do. Dangerous and risky tasks will be assigned to robots. Jobs such as climbing ladders, working in high places, checking for the presence of noxious chemicals in chemical and fuel storage tanks, and driving vehicles under dangerous conditions will all be robot jobs. Gradually, the robots will be able to take over many jobs, but in the interim, they will take on the role of a reliable personal assistant to current employees.

I predict that in the future (the next 10 years), jobs will consist of mostly monitoring tasks. Whether the task is sitting in the cab of a self-driving truck monitoring the data as the truck moves down the road, monitoring manufacturing robots from an office above the manufacturing floor, monitoring stock market computers, or monitoring computers that are advising wealthy bank customers on how to manage their money, monitoring jobs will be widespread. Eventually, robots not only will do most of the work but also will monitor the monitoring. This possibility may appear sooner than a lot of people expect because a current headline just published reads, "One of the Biggest Bond Market Players Has No Employees."

Ironically, technology will present new problems for companies that are not behaviorally sophisticated. Technology typically reduces the natural positive reinforcement in most jobs. The active behaviors in jobs today provide much of the daily reinforcement for employees. Finding a file, corresponding with customers, making calls, and sending e-mails all have a visible completion that is reinforcing to most employees. When modern machines take over, these tasks will be done without human assistance leaving only monitoring robot activity for the human employee. Because of the high reliability of robots, there will be very few interventions in the job. This will cause all the problems produced by low frequencies of reinforcement—boredom, inattention, high rates of distraction, and extinction of key job behaviors that are still left for humans to do.

Low levels of job reinforcement also cause employees to seek reinforcement elsewhere. They may seek transfers to other jobs in the company or seek employment outside the company. Because distractibility is high under low reinforcement, use of phones, tablets, and other devices will pull employees away from attending to job-related tasks. Job extinction

$$R = k \frac{r}{r + r_e}$$

Figure 18-1   The matching law.
Key: R = response or target behavior; k = asymptote or highest rate known or possible; r = reinforcers for R, the target or on-task behavior or response; r_e (called "r sub e") = reinforcement for behavior other than that of the target or on-task behavior

potentially will cause quality, safety, and cost problems because no one will be paying attention to the actual work.

The matching law is very helpful in managing behavior affected by technological advances in the workplace. Discovered by Dr. Richard Herrnstein of Harvard University, the matching law is one of the most robust formulas in behavior analysis. The formula is highly predictive. It states, in a nutshell, that behavior goes to the most reinforcing part of the environment. Figure 18-1 shows the matching law.

Under low levels of reinforcement, if the employee monitoring a process hears a door open (r_e), she will turn toward the door. Most monitoring of computers and robots is really boring because there are few problems that require human attention. If someone enters the room, the task of monitoring equipment (or processes) likely will be neglected for the more reinforcing conversation (r_e) with the visitor. If there are no visitors, the person is likely to text, call, or read something more interesting than monitoring the equipment or process. When the person is alone, surfing the web will be an even more popular pastime. By assigning the value of 1 to k, you can see how reinforcement increases or decreases on-task behavior. For example, in today's workplace, reinforcement for behavior that is not on-task (r_e) is increasing substantially more than reinforcement for on-task behavior (r). Almost 1,000 new apps are accepted every working day by Apple alone. Off the job reinforcement is advancing at a much higher rate than job reinforcement. The practical impact of this is that supervisors and managers must increase reinforcement on the job just to remain at current performance levels. With r_e at low levels, it takes very little reinforcement to maintain performance levels. However, in today's workplace, it is almost impossible to eliminate extraneous reinforcement (r_e) unless you control all changes in the environment, including sound, movement, and visual changes that cause distractions. Thus the only option for business is to increase work-related reinforcement. Unfortunately, this formula is relatively unknown in business circles and business literature, but the ability to analyze these problems and take corrective action is becoming increasingly important in a technological-drove future.

Training and Technology

As modern business is experiencing ever-increasing rates of change, it is imperative to find ways to teach employees new skills more efficiently and to have them perform at high rates quicker. It is common in many businesses that before employees become fully proficient in the current processes, procedures, or technology, new ones come along to replace them. This means that businesses rarely experience the return on investment they have come to expect from an "old" technology before a new one is introduced.

It also means that because of the short life span of any given procedure, method, or technology, human performance will rarely be maximized and often only rises to mediocre levels before the next change occurs. Indeed, if it were not for the increase in efficiency of the new technologies, we would actually be losing ground because of slow learning rates produced by traditional training methods.

Everyone is experiencing the problems associated with poor performance on new equipment and processes. All of us have waited patiently in a department store because the clerk had not yet developed the skill to use the latest software upgrade. Often, when the computer is down, even simple tasks can't be performed because the performer hasn't been taught an alternative way to complete the job.

The modern technology that organizations really need is the one that will enable people to learn quickly (in a fraction of "normal" learning times), perform at high rates, and retain what they learn for long periods of time. Peter Senge, in *The Fifth Discipline: The Art and Practice of the Learning Organization* (Doubleday, 1990), has made a case for the *learning* organization. He suggests that in the future, the most successful organizations will not be the ones with the most innovative products or the best marketing campaigns. Rather,

> the most successful companies will be the ones that can most efficiently train their workforces to assimilate and use vast amounts of ever-changing information.

This means that modern organizations must develop a culture where people look forward to change—one where people want to, and can, learn new things and learn them quickly. Humans have the ability to learn new habits quickly but need changes in the way they are taught.

Traditional Educational Processes—A Poor Model for Rapidly Changing Businesses

The effectiveness of American education has changed little since the mid-1980s when B. F. Skinner wrote an article entitled, "The Shame of American Education." The shame to which Skinner referred was not the fact that we had the knowledge and technology to double learning rates in 1984 but rather that the know-how had already existed for 30 years. Over 30 years have passed since he wrote that article, and we certainly have not doubled the rates of learning but are worse off today than in 1954.

Although most parents are dissatisfied with the ineffectiveness of the schools, businesses use the same ineffective methods employed by public schools. The way we transfer knowledge throughout the world has not changed in centuries.

In an effort to differentiate itself from public education, business has resorted to calling what it does "adult learning," as though adults learn in a different way than children. This reveals how little business knows about how people learn. Everyone, young or old, learns from his or her environment. Each one of us is different in that we all have had different experiences. As different as we are from one another, we all learn the same way—from interacting with our environment.

Ray Kurzweil[2] predicts that in the years ahead, employees will spend most of their time acquiring new knowledge. He seems to base this prediction on the current inefficient methods of transferring knowledge. With technology changing almost daily, what you learned last week will be outdated this week. At any rate, I agree with Kurzweil because the rate of change will require constant training to just to keep up.

Constant change will turn traditional education on its head or will lead to apps and software to make even monitoring by humans largely unnecessary. The problem for businesses is that given the inefficiency of traditional training, employees will spend the most of their time updating their knowledge of how to use existing technology or in creating new technology. Clearly, the organizations that are able to train employees to a level of fluency in the shortest time will succeed where the others will be left behind. Think of shopping at an electronics retailer and having salespeople who can't answer your questions about a new product.

The current model of training in business is to spend days or weeks in a classroom and months of training on the job. In the future, the ability of a business to transfer knowledge efficiently will be a measure of the chances of its survival. In the future, on-the-job training will be a luxury that business can't afford. Some, should I say many, jobs now require months of on-the-job training, in addition to training received in the classroom, for employees to become proficient. Even clerical training on new products and services will need updating almost monthly.

Until the robots take over, people will still be a major factor in all types of business. In the immediate future, people will be needed to market, manufacture, transport, and sell products and services. Not understanding how to create work environments that bring out the best in people will increasingly put such companies at a competitive disadvantage, and they may not be here when the robots arrive.

Fortunately, technology and the science of behavior have combined to make possible the fluent training of employees in a fraction of the time it now takes to learn something new. Dr. Ogden Lindsley,[3] a pioneer in behavior analysis, led the way in discovering methods of teaching that are far superior to traditional methods. He developed this method of teaching—called *precision teaching*—in the mid-1950s. Although more than 60 years have passed since early demonstrations of its effectiveness, only a few places are using the approach today, which proves the saying, "Just because something works doesn't mean that people will do it." And "Just because something doesn't work doesn't mean that people will not continue to do it."

Education—Back to the Future

Educational programs tout "active learning" as a feature of their materials. How else do we learn? We are active either in the classroom or outside it. Remember, we learn from interacting with our environment. Passive learning is a myth. The more active the learner, the more the student learns.

When educators complain that something is lacking in this kind of education, my response is, "Let's pinpoint what the student needs to do and build a fluency program to teach it." All the research shows that the amount of practice in typical schools is woefully lacking in all subjects.

Before the student is fluent in one thing, the teacher moves to another. In the class where a teacher is more concerned about covering the lesson than what the student learns, few actually learn. If the normal curve is an accurate reflection of student achievement, this means that less than half of students learn enough to be successful with the material that follows. I believe that a passing grade of C is immoral because with each passing grade the child has less and less of a chance of becoming fluent with anything academic.

Learning and rate of learning are facilitated by the amount of correct responding. In order to become fluent in a subject, you not only are able to get a correct response but you are also able to recall it quickly. Lindsley's goal was that a student would double learning each week. In America's public schools, the rate of learning is probably less than 10 percent of the material per week.

Schneider (1985) trained college students to outperform three-year veteran air-traffic controllers in 40 hours. Using technology, his students were able to respond to problems or questions over 32,000 times in the 40-hour training session. After six months with no further practice, the students were still performing at a rate equal to the experienced controllers.

Fluency technology is not used widely in business, but where it is being used, it is showing spectacular successes. However, I strongly suggest that business owners begin to look seriously at fluency technology to meet the ever-increasing training needs of their employees.

Response Cost

Inventions that require effort on the part of the user or, to put it technically, have a high response cost will also receive limited success because there are very few people who will go to the trouble to use any invention that requires extra work. Many inventors, not understanding behavior analysis, waste a lot of time and money inventing things and processes that are only novel antecedents and soon fade from the commercial scene. This is so because they don't know the role of consequences in learning, often focusing only on the antecedent side of the behavior change model and misunderstanding the effect of consequences on learning.

In fact, many studies show that use of a product is negatively affected by the amount of effort it takes to use that product. If one website requires three clicks of the mouse to purchase a product and another requires only one click, the one-click company will eventually win. Amazon does a very good job of expediting the purchasing and delivery processes and is highly successful because of it.

An example of misunderstanding the effect of effort on product use is the health app on every iPhone 6. Only those who have a peculiar reinforcement history will find pleasure in inputting all the data, calories, body function measures, and other information that the app requires to give you a valid fitness analysis.

Most new products don't even come with an instruction manual because using the product is so simple. Manuals are available only on the web because they are only needed for special problem solving or for those who want to know every detail of the operation of the product. Successful products allow the purchaser to unpack the product and begin using it immediately with no training. Cell phones are so easy to use and produce so many positive reinforcers that they are almost impossible to ignore even when they put the user at risk. When they ring, buzz, or emit a tone or other signal indicating that someone wants to talk to you or has sent you a message, the desire to look is almost irresistible no matter where you are.

Many older people think that young people are too impulsive and want instant gratification. Of course, older people would be the same way if the same technology were available when they were young. It's human nature.

In the end, if a new invention comes on the market and saves the user time and effort (PICs), you can bet it will succeed unless another can save more time and effort. Future products and services that deliver the most PICs to the customer will win in the marketplace. Producers of products and services need to understand how technology, human behavior, and learning interact to create outcomes that are good for the employee and the organization.

Notes

1. Kobi Vortman, "InSightec: The Operating Room of the Future." Lecture delivered at the Diane Sherman Prize Ceremony for Medical Innovations for a Better World, Technion—Israel Institute of Technology, June 9, 2013.
2. Ray Kurzweil (1990). *The Age of Spiritual Machines*, Penguin Books, New York.
3. O. R. Lindsley (1992). "Why Aren't Effective Teaching Tools Widely Adopted?" *Journal of Applied Behavior Analysis* 25:21–26.

19

Getting Smarter Quicker

*Organizations learn only through
individuals who learn.*
　　　—Peter Senge, *The Fifth Discipline*

Hopefully, by this point in this book you have some ideas about how you would create an organization such as the one described by Senge. The problem still remains that even if employees want to learn more, they may not be able to learn at a rate that will keep the organization ahead of the competition. Traditional educational methods certainly have little to offer to solve this dilemma.

What Is Wrong with Traditional Education?

Probably nowhere in modern society are there more opportunities for improved efficiency and effectiveness than in American education. Training methods in business are no more efficient, but their inefficiency is usually hidden by the fact that considerable time learning to use what was presented in the classroom is done in on-the-job training.

There is no point in reciting all the problems of modern education in America. The poor showing of U.S. education in comparison with the other major economies of the world is well known. It has been documented too frequently, and still nothing seems to change.[1] Even though by many measures of our economy and standard of living, we outperform almost all countries, if we continue to lag behind educationally, it can only have negative effects on both.

The promise of technology in improving education at work and at school has yet to be realized. In my opinion, this is not because computers can't increase learning rates substantially but because those who design educational software and those who use computers to teach often don't really understand what learning is all about. So-called computer-assisted instruction (CAI) often turns out to be nothing more than a fancy page turner with beautiful graphics for the students, adding little that they couldn't get from reading an "old-fashioned" book and less than they could get from an "old-fashioned" lecture. At least in the old-fashioned lecture, students could ask questions! Even though the word *interactive* is appearing more and more in educational settings and with commercial learning companies, if education is not truly interactive, it doesn't teach much. There are still too many educators who believe that the solution to student learning lies in more hours in the school day, more days in the school year, and smaller classes. Unfortunately, this kind of thinking does not encourage considering new ways of increasing the efficiency and effectiveness of teaching methods. In fact, there has been a consistent reluctance on the part of the education community to examine teaching methods.

Siegfried Engelmann, professor at the University of Oregon, wrote *War Against the Schools' Academic Child Abuse*, a book that should be of interest to anyone who cares about education.[2] He defines *academic child abuse* as "the use of practices that cause unnecessary failure." Engelmann cites two studies that deserve to be repeated here. Coles (1978) reviewed approximately 1,000 research studies on "learning disabilities." Not *one* considered the relationship between instruction or other school factors and the learning disability! Similarly, Alessi (1988) discovered that of about 5,000 children referred by school psychologists for remedial education, not one case was considered to be the fault of the curriculum, the teaching practices, or the school administration.

Consider these findings against the following quote by Engelmann:

> During the years that I've worked with kids and teachers, I have never seen a kid with an IQ of over 80 that could not be taught to

read in a timely manner (one school year), and I've worked directly or indirectly (as a trainer) with thousands of them. I've never seen a kid that could not be taught arithmetic and language skills. During these years, however, I've become increasingly intolerant of reforms formulated by naïve spectators who don't really understand what school failure is and how it can be reversed.

Cathy Watkins[3] summarizes the problem by saying:

Suggestions about how to address the problems of education have included changing the content of instruction, raising educational standards, increasing the amount of instructional time, increasing pay for teachers, and a long list of other "solutions" that would change just about every structural and functional aspect of education except *how children are taught*.

The traditional method of teaching has changed little since about the eleventh century and usually works as follows:

1. The teacher or instructor presents material to the class as a group.
2. The teacher or instructor asks a few questions, which only a few students get a chance to answer.
3. The opportunity is there, usually, to do a couple of problems in class or work through an example.
4. The homework or study assignments are given, where some practice sometimes occurs.
5. The students are eventually tested, and if they score a passing grade, usually about 70 percent, they are considered to have learned the material.

Business has basically adopted this same model. The only difference is that the homework is on-the-job training (OJT). Typical of training in business settings is the training that I received when I was learning to use basic computer software. Even though we were all on the computer, the teaching model required that we all stay together in learning. This was a most inefficient method because some in the room had considerable experience with computers and others had none. This procedure is reminiscent of a quote from Skinner in *Walden Two*,[4] which discusses the use of grade levels in schools: "The grade is an administrative device which does violence to the nature of the developmental process."

The instructor would show us her computer screen using a liquid-crystal display (LCD) projector and walk us through each step. She would then check each person's computer to see whether the student had done it correctly. Once everyone had completed that assignment satisfactorily, she would show us another feature. While in the classroom, I thought I had a clear understanding of how to do things. However, by the time I got back to my office, I could not do most of what she covered in class without referring to the manual or asking someone in the office for help. With so little practice, retention of the material was impossible.

Many people would respond to my situation by saying, "Of course. Isn't that the way it is supposed to be done? She taught you; now the rest is up to you." I remember my college history professor telling my freshman class, "Going to college is like going to the drugstore and ordering a soda. The soda jerk can fix you the very best soda he knows how, but whether you drink it is up to you." He then proceeded to read from the same old musty yellow notes that he had first written back in 1912.

This model of teaching is inefficient in both business and academic settings. To be sure, most students eventually learn, but the problem is, *How many learn, how much do they learn, and at what rate do they learn?* To put the problem in some perspective, let's revisit Morningside Academy, a private school in Seattle, Washington, that I discussed in Chapter 16.

The Morningside Model

Dr. Kent Johnson, founder of Morningside Academy, estimates that core academic content from kindergarten through the twelfth grade could be taught easily in six years. In his school, which is designed primarily for children who have had problems in regular schools, students achieve at a rate four to six times the national average.

Dr. Johnson opened Morningside Academy in 1980. He has maintained meticulous records of actual learning since that time. He has to do so because he gives parents a written money-back guarantee that their child will advance the equivalent of two grade levels in their worst subject every year. Since 1980, less than 1 percent of parents have requested their money back because the average achievement at Morningside is 2.4 grade levels per year. Such gains have been increasing since 1980, and it is now common for the school average on some subjects to increase over three grades per year, as measured by the California Achievement Test. Contrast those figures with the national average of less than one grade level per year!

The school's results are equally impressive with adults. Adults who tested between second- and eighth-grade levels in reading on entering Morningside training gained at a rate of 1.7 grades per 20 hours of instruction. The U.S. standard is one grade per 100 hours of instruction. How does Morningside do it?

Fluency

In 1967, the U.S. government funded a program, *Project Follow-Through*, to compare a wide range of teaching methods with the goal of finding effective methods for educating disadvantaged children. The results showed that the methods known as *direct instruction* and *behavior analysis* came in first and second, respectively, among 22 different approaches tried.[5] The traditional classroom method came in dead last. As incredible as it might seem, the outcome of this research was that funds were provided to improve the traditional method rather than adopt any of the methods that demonstrated academic superiority!

At Morningside, Dr. Johnson combined direct instruction and behavior analysis to form a teaching method that he calls the *Morningside model of generative instruction*.[6] Dr. Engelmann, mentioned previously, developed the direct instruction (DI) technique.[7] DI is carefully scripted both in the order of presentation of the academic material and in the words the teacher uses during instruction. Through systematic analysis, Engelmann has been able to determine the most effective presentation and sequencing of the material.

The behavior analysis approach added measurement, feedback, and positive reinforcement to Engelmann's material. In addition, Dr. Johnson used a technique developed by Dr. Ogden Lindsley of the University of Kansas (see Chapter 18). Dr. Lindsley named this method *fluency*.

Fluency is automatic, nonhesitant responding. If people are fluent in a particular subject, they do not have to think about what they are doing, and they can respond quickly and accurately after long periods of no instruction. They are also able to respond for extended periods with less fatigue and can generalize what they have learned to novel situations. This is what Dr. Johnson calls *learning for free*.

To attain fluency, responding at high rates is required. Because the method deals with measurable, observable behavior, the rates necessary to attain fluency can be determined for any academic subject. For example, certain basic math concepts such as addition, subtraction, multiplication, and division may require a student to be able to do as many as 80 math facts a minute with no errors. Some students can do up to 120 a minute. Although Morningside concentrates on basic skills, it also teaches such subjects as problem solving and fluent thinking skills.

Because practice is the hallmark of fluency training, a Morningside classroom hour is divided as follows: 10 minutes of instruction, 40 minutes of practice, and 10 minutes of break. By the way, students have no homework. The average teacher may not be able to relate to this model of classroom instruction because it is so different from the way traditional classroom teaching is done. This model seeks to determine the minimum amount of information that needs to be given to allow the maximum time for active involvement of the student with the material.

Dr. Johnson's methods also have been applied in regular schools with impressive results. He has developed a model of individualized instruction that is manageable and effective for public education. However, the move to adopt it by the traditional educational community is very slow.

The work of Johnson and others has made one thing very clear: to learn efficiently, learners must have the opportunity for high rates of interaction with the material to be learned or the skill to be mastered. We know this is true because a high frequency of learner response dramatically increases the amount of positive reinforcement the learner can receive for her or his efforts—and *positive reinforcement will accelerate learning*.

Sources of Reinforcement

Where does all this reinforcement come from? Clearly, no teacher or instructor can provide positive reinforcement for every learner behavior. In fact, the reinforcement comes from the students seeing or knowing that they got the correct answer. In most of our learning histories, external reinforcers have been paired with correct answers to the point that getting an answer correct is reinforcing to almost everyone. Therefore, students given many opportunities to answer questions correctly will have an opportunity for high rates of reinforcement quite independent of the social reinforcement they might get from the teachers, parents, or other students. A big part of the fluency model depends on high rates of correct responding. Nothing is more reinforcing than doing well, and students of all ages who get the opportunity to perform successfully at high frequency will be highly reinforced. This high level of positive reinforcement will accelerate learning to rates that surprise most students.

One of the criticisms of fluency techniques that has come from traditional educators is that it smacks of "rote learning," and as I have been told many times by school staff, "Rote learning went out 30 years ago." My response to them is that maybe it is not coincidental that learning rates in schools have been going down for the last 30 years as well! Of course, in my day, rote learning was accomplished by drill, and the drill was accomplished by negative reinforcement. Under such conditions, students would not be excited about learning. However, when drills and other rote-learning methods are coupled with positive reinforcement, students beg to do them.

A number of years ago, one of our industrial clients asked me if I would share what his workers were learning about fluency and positive reinforcement with a local school. Of course, I said that I would. The school selected six teachers to pilot positive reinforcement methods in their classes. To give the method a fair test, we chose teachers who varied in their enthusiasm to try these techniques. At a review I conducted after several weeks, one of the older teachers was still a little skeptical about this new approach. As I was talking to the group, I said, "You will really have it made when your students beg you to test them." Toward the end of that school year, that teacher sent me a card. It read simply, "Dr. Daniels, I really have it made!"

None of the criticisms of this approach that I have seen advanced by traditional educators has been supported by credible research. However, research support for fluency as an effective method of learning is coming from several unrelated sources.

Motor Performance Research

Richard A. Schmidt, in *Motor Learning and Performance*,[8] says that in most motor learning, about 300 repetitions under the most favorable conditions are required to produce automaticity. He says, "Automatic responding can develop with several hundred trials of practice under the most favorable conditions, but it appears that many more trials than this are needed in less optimal real-world settings."

Schmidt notes advantages to automaticity similar to those discovered quite separately by researchers working on fluency. He writes, "This capability to produce skills automatically means that component parts (e.g., dribbling and running in basketball) do not require much attention, which then frees attention for other important elements in a game (where to pass) or for style or form in dance. Also, automatic processes are faster than controlled processes, allowing the performer to respond more quickly and with certainty."

Walter Schneider (1985), mentioned in the last chapter, made similar discoveries. In training air-traffic controllers, he found that in training them to rapidly visualize flight patterns, "we compress simulated time by a factor of 100; for example, making a judgment of where an aircraft should turn (a maneuver that normally takes about 5 minutes) would take about 0.5 second. *By compressing time in this way, we can provide the trainee with more trials at executing this particular component in a single day of training than he or she could get in a year of training with conventional methods*" (emphasis added). He further states, "Active participation is enhanced if subjects need to respond every few seconds."

Fortunately, technology and the science of behavior have combined to make possible the fluent training of employees in a fraction of the time it now takes to learn something new.

Expertise Research

Anders Ericsson[9] at Florida State University has conducted extensive research on the acquisition of expertise. Over the last 20+ years, he has investigated expertise in every field in which there are objective ways to separate experts from others. His list of fields includes chess, music, sports, medicine, engineering, and ballet.

There is an amazing consistency to what Ericsson has discovered about what it takes to become an expert in any field of endeavor. He has discovered that it takes a minimum of 10 years of deliberate practice to become an expert at anything. Ericsson's investigations have revealed that anyone who has attained expert status has engaged in at least 10,000 hours of deliberate practice. This amounts to an average of 20 hours of practice for 50 weeks a year over the course of 10 years.

One of his findings that flies in the face of popular notions about high performers is that at least 96 percent of the variance in performance is accounted for by deliberate practice alone. Another way of saying this is that less than 4 percent of an expert's performance is due to all other factors, including something often referred to as "natural talent." This is a very important finding for anyone who wants to become an expert at anything. This means that almost anyone who wants to excel at something needs to engage in deliberate practice for 10,000 hours. In his new book, *Peak*,[10] Ericsson points out that this must be deliberate practice—that is, a concerted effort to improve one's skill. (Unfortunately for me, four hours on the golf course doesn't count as deliberate practice.)

It becomes clear from the research in all these areas that the number of reinforced repetitions is a very important element in teaching and learning. Although the relationship between speed and number of trials is not fully understood, the fact is clear that more repetitions lead to more reinforcement, which leads to faster learning, greater retention, the ability to generalize to novel situations, and the ability to perform under stressful and distracting circumstances. What manager in any organization would not want that?

As noted earlier, the research of Ericsson, Engelmann, and Johnson and Layng suggests that most failures in learning are actually failures in teaching methods, not the result of student motivation and/or ability. This finding has tremendous implications for business, industry, and government. It means that most performance problems are not because the performer is incapable of performing at a high level but are caused by either poor training, lack of a reinforcing environment, or both.

We see in most organizations that many performance problems can be addressed successfully and economically by employing teaching methods that involve high rates of responding and frequent reinforcement. Some of this is being done already.

For an example of what fluency techniques can accomplish in business, let me tell you about an application at a Delta Faucet plant in Tennessee. Delta opened a new plant, and it was important for the company to train a large number of people in a short period of time to assemble faucets quickly and correctly. By developing a computer training program based on the fluency technology, the company was able to reduce learning time from 24 hours plus extensive OJT to fewer than 10 hours plus only 1 hour of OJT. The first assembly teams went to the line having never seen a faucet part except on the computer training system, and they successfully built their first faucet in 42 minutes! Bill Hampton, human resources manager, said that each one-half hour spent in fluency training was the equivalent of three to four hours of hands-on training on the assembly line.

Blue Cross Blue Shield of Georgia used fluency-building techniques to teach clerks medical terminology. Previous classroom training lasted for three days with no real concept of what students learned or retained from the training. Deficiencies in training were soon discovered when the trainees returned to the workplace, and the company opted for a fluency implementation. Using a computer programmed for fluency training, all the students performed to criteria in fewer than five hours. These results are typical, not extraordinary.

Recently, a large healthcare provider used an accelerated learning program my team developed and reduced total training time for billing clerks from six to three months. Also, the new clerks achieved fluency in their tasks during the training, which allowed them to generate correct billing statements the first day on the job. The company expects that this training will result in a savings of $4.5 million.

Accelerated learning is not a thing of the future. It is available now. Organizations faced with the need to train more people more often should avail themselves of this powerful educational method. The educational community, having less pressure to teach more in a shorter period of time will be, unfortunately, slower to adopt these methods. In the meantime, businesses will have to continue to do the educators' jobs for them. Because of the demonstrated effectiveness and efficiency of these techniques, business and government not only should use them—but they should encourage local schools to do likewise.

The following observation, written in 1988, supports the need for revamping our education methods:

> There must be an "industrial revolution" in education, in which educational science and the ingenuity of educational technology combine to modernize the grossly inefficient and clumsy procedures of conventional education. Work in the schools of the future will be marvelously though simply organized, so as to adjust almost automatically to individual differences and the characteristics of the learning process. There will be many laborsaving schemes and devices, and even machines—not at all for the mechanizing of edu-

cation, but for the freeing of teacher and pupil from educational drudgery and incompetence.[11]

This paragraph could have been written today. It is no less applicable to schools and business. The current model of training in business is to spend days or weeks in a classroom and months of training on the job. OJT is fast becoming a luxury that business can't afford, and in the near future, the ability of a business to transfer knowledge efficiently will be a critical measure of survival.

Notes

1. A. D. Miller and W. L. Heward, "Do Your Students Really Know Their Math Facts?" *Intervention in School and Clinic* 28: 98–104; and P. Wingert, "The Sum of Mediocrity," *Newsweek*, December 6, 1996, p. 96.
2. Siegfried Engelmann, *War Against the Schools' Academic Child Abuse* (Portland, OR: Halcyon House, 1992).
3. Cathy L. Watkins, *Project Follow-Through: A Case Study of Contingencies Influencing Instructional Practices of the Educational Establishment* (Cambridge, MA: Cambridge Center for Behavioral Studies, 1997).
4. B. F. Skinner, *Walden Two* (Indianapolis: Hackett Publishing Company, 2005).
5. Watkins, *Project Follow-Through*.
6. K. R. Johnson and T. V. J. Layng, "Breaking the Structuralist Barrier: Literacy and Numeracy with Fluency," *American Psychologist* 47 (1992): 1475–1490.
7. S. Engelmann and D. W. Carnine, *Theory of Instruction* (New York: Irvington, 1982).
8. Richard A. Schmidt, *Motor Learning and Performance: From Principles to Practice* (Windsor, Ontario, Canada: Human Kinetics, 1991).
9. K. Anders Ericsson and Neil Charness, "Expert Performance: Its Structure and Acquisition," *American Psychologist*, August 1994, pp. 725–747.
10. Anders Ericsson and Robert Pool, *Peak: Secrets from the New Science of Expertise* (New York: Eamon Dolan/Houghton Mifflin Harcourt, 2016).
11. L. T. Benjamin, "A History of Teaching Machines," *American Psychologist* 43(1988): 703–712.

20
Performance Management
The Executive Function

If you think this is easy,
you are doing it wrong.

Edward Gibbon, an English historian, said, "The winds and waves are always on the side of the ablest navigator." I interpret this to mean that the sailor who thoroughly understands the winds and the ocean currents will have few problems sailing a ship in the desired direction. Changing conditions don't present insurmountable obstacles for expert sailors, just additional opportunities for them to exercise their skill. If the winds shift or the tide changes, the expert sailor simply modifies the sails and moves the rudder to adapt to changing conditions.

To the executive who understands human behavior, changing business conditions don't present problems, just additional opportunities to exercise his or her skill. In my opinion, if *the CEO doesn't know the science of human behavior and how to apply it to leadership, he or she will have great difficulty surviving the next 10 years and puts his or her company at financial risk.* I'm convinced that as executives understand and implement the principles set forth in this book, they'll make dramatic gains in the performance and profitability of their companies.

The Executive Role in Performance Management

Executives should learn and apply every performance management technique described in this book, but because of their positions in their organizations, they have some additional responsibilities.

Results/Behavior Selection

It is the responsibility of a company's executives to pinpoint the desired organizational results. Once this is determined, the executives should make sure that the pinpointed results fit the values of the organization.

This task should be value driven. Value driven brings up questions like "What are acceptable and unacceptable ways to get results here? Is it results at any cost? If not, what are the limits? How are they determined? What are our guiding principles and values?"

Although values are not usually stated in pinpointed terms, it is only by pinpointing them that you can ensure that your organization lives by them. Concepts such as honesty, teamwork, innovativeness, concern for people, customer service, commitment to quality, and so on can and should be defined in behavioral terms. In fact, if you can't define your organization's values in terms of specific behaviors, they will be practically useless in helping you to accomplish your mission. Many executives think this shouldn't be necessary, but in recent times, executives have been imprisoned because their employees thought what they were doing to get results was acceptable.

The ultimate purpose of including this task as a part of a mission statement is to determine which behaviors are acceptable and which are unacceptable. This task involves some discussion of behaviors.

A vice president of one of our largest clients recently asked me, "How do you think we're doing with our quality management program?"

I said, "Some are doing well, and some are not doing so well."

"Who's not doing well?" he then asked.

"I can't tell you," I replied.

Looking puzzled, he asked, "Why not?"

"Because," I continued, "*one of the managers who isn't doing anything to support quality management just got promoted.*" I refused to single out this manager because it was obvious that he had done everything that *really* mattered to the way the organization was run. The organization *said* that quality management was important, but its actions indicated that it actually valued other behaviors more. Until the executives in this company decide which behaviors are important and which are not, they will continue to have spotty success implementing any new technology.

After determining organizational results, the task of determining organizational values and their associated behaviors should be a high priority with executive management. This task should come before all other executive responsibilities, including those that directly affect profit. The executive cannot exercise true financial responsibility if profit is attained by behaviors that are self-serving, wasteful, or repressive—not to mention illegal, unethical, or immoral.

Systems and Structures

Executives have the responsibility for designing the organization's systems and structures. These elements affect behavior in general ways. For example, if a vice president of sales establishes revenue goals, the sales staff will try to meet those goals. If, in addition, she asks for a certain number of new accounts, the sales staff will spend time prospecting for new accounts in addition to simply trying to maximize revenues from a few good customers. These rules or structures affect what the sales staff does from day to day.

However, if that same sales executive provides bonuses only for revenues, independent of whether they come from an old or a new account, the message of what is really important will be determined by the consequences associated with it. No matter how clearly the goal is communicated or how important it is said to be, performance will be determined more by what is reinforced and rewarded than by what is said. First and foremost, executives must be sure that all systems and structures link reinforcement to the behaviors they want and only to the behaviors they want.

One of our recent customers worked very hard to deploy our behavior-based safety system. Protecting employees from injury and even death was very important to this company because it was engaged in dangerous work involving heavy moving equipment. The company diligently trained a large number of employees as observers of work behavior. It set up an accurate measuring system to track the increase in safe behavior on the job through frequent observations. In addition, it celebrated the improvements resulting from changes in critical behaviors—fewer accidents, less lost time, and fewer injuries. In other words, the company established meaningful structures that set the stage for making sure that safe behavior was reinforced and rewarded. The company was successful, but it did not achieve the highest levels of safety until it also involved first-line supervisors in the process. What the supervisors were trained to do was to comment on and actively support the observers for observing safe behavior on the job. When supervisors were reinforced for reinforcing observers who were present when the behaviors were occurring, the number of safe behaviors increased dramatically, and safe behavior soon became the norm.

In an organization of any significant size, senior executives can never personally deliver enough reinforcement to affect frontline employee behavior. Therefore, they must make sure that the systems and structures facilitate and positively reinforce the behavior of supervisors, team leaders, and peers. They must be reinforced for knowing what to reinforce, who to reinforce, and how to reinforce effectively. Ensuring that formal organizational systems and structures support day-to-day reinforcement is the most important role an executive can play in maximizing performance in an organization.

Reinforcer/Reward Selection

Reinforcer and reward selection is ultimately determined by the performers in the company, that is, how they respond to attempts at reinforcing and rewarding behaviors and celebrating results. However, executives should define the limits of the reinforcers and rewards available for managers and supervisors to use. Is time off allowed as a reward? If so, how much? Extra breaks? How many? Can money be used? If so, how much? What about celebrations? Do we need to give supervisors a budget for reinforcement and reward activities? What are the limits on how big, how extravagant, and where celebrations will be held?

Although the boundaries should be broadly defined, it's helpful for people throughout the organization to know the limits. If executives spend some time on these issues, they will minimize troublesome surprises that may surface later.

Reinforcer/Reward Distribution

The prime consideration in reinforcer/reward distribution is to make sure that your system is noncompetitive. All systems affecting human performance should be monitored to identify and eliminate contingencies that create internal competition. *Reinforcement should multiply opportunities for more reinforcement, not reduce them.* That is, one person's reinforcement and reward should increase the chances that others will be reinforced. If one performer finds a better way to do something, would that individual automatically share his or her discovery with all the others who do the same thing? Where there is competition for reinforcement, performers are reluctant to share discoveries that might give them a performance advantage.

As explained in Chapter 16, the second consideration is that there is a direct linkage between the behaviors and the reward. Reward systems such as bonuses, profit sharing, and gain sharing should be tied to individual performance, not to some mathematical formula that is applied to all performers in a job category. There should be measurement of what each person actually does to add value to the company.

Reinforcer/Reward Effectivenes

Executives have the overall responsibility for ensuring that performance is managed effectively. This encompasses all corporate performance, including initiatives such as continuous improvement, behavior-based safety, reengineering, and so on.

It's important for executives to understand techniques of evaluating performance such as multiple-baseline, ABA, and other research designs to make sure that they get their money's worth from their investments. Internal performance management personnel should have the responsibility to evaluate and report on the investment status and make recommendations to executives about continuing any initiatives, increasing their use, or pulling the plug. All such decisions should be data based. The final evaluation should be based on results data, not just on behaviors or counts of behaviors or even anecdotal evidence.

Herrnstein's Hyperbola—The Matching Law

This was described earlier, but it is of particular importance for the CEO or president to know. Remember, the *matching law* shows that people allocate their behaviors to tasks in proportion to the relative amount of reinforcement available for each task. To put this more simply, behavior follows the relative frequency of reinforcement. If there is little reinforcement for a given task (task A), as in completing paperwork, and much more in talking to a coworker or e-mailing or texting a friend (task B), the employee will leave task A and spend time doing task B. What Dr. Herrnstein's work means for the executive is that every time you introduce a new corporate initiative, you potentially dilute effort on existing initiatives. In other words, when someone spends more time and effort doing something new, that person will have less time to spend on some previous behavior. However, if a new initiative is introduced with no reinforcement, little time will be spent with it because reinforcement will continue to occur for the old ways of doing things.

Following is a summary of what Dr. Herrnstein's research discovered:

1. Noncontingent reinforcement typically dilutes job focus and accomplishment.
2. When there's little reinforcement for doing a job, it takes only a little extraneous reinforcement (r_e) to pull someone off the task.
3. When there's an increase in non-job-related reinforcement, it takes an *increase* in job-related positive reinforcement to *maintain the same level* of job-related effort.
4. If you introduce any new program or system without concentrated, planned reinforcement, you will get only minimum participation in that program or system because of the large amount of reinforcement still existing for prior behaviors.

Executive Behaviors

MBWA Through the Chain of Command

Management by wandering around (MBWA) was popularized in the book *In Search of Excellence* (HarperCollins, 2004) by Thomas J. Peters and Robert H. Waterman, Jr. Although the acronym is not used very much these days, the concept is very relevant to today's management. You can't see many behaviors in an office. The executive must make sure that managers allow supervisors enough time to observe employees at work. The observations are to help employees coach, reinforce, and hear their ideas for improvement and get feedback on how any changes are helping or hindering performance. MBWA is a good thing to do only if you understand the purpose of being in the place where work is actually taking place. Tom Peters encouraged executives to get out into the work area because he saw this being done in the best companies.

Dr. Judy Komaki (1986) would make the same suggestion, but for a different reason. Her research has shown that the best managers spend more time in the work area *because it makes for the most effective delivery of positive reinforcement.*

Peters told executives to get out and see what's going on. What they did while they were out there was left to chance. A plant manager once told me, "I wish I could get my hands on that Peters guy. I'd pinch his head off. Ever since my boss read that book, he's in the plant all the time! You can tell where he's been by the smoke from the fires he sets. He upsets people wherever he goes."

One thing we don't need these days is more executives wandering around reinforcing the wrong behaviors or inadvertently delivering punishment. The potential problem with MBWA is that most executives and upper-level managers don't know what they're looking at when they do go out and wander around on the plant or office floor. I sometimes call this form of MBWA "management by *wondering* around," as in "I wonder why this person is doing that," "I wonder why that person is not working," and "I wonder why that machine isn't running." Because their sampling of behavior is limited to a minute or two on a very infrequent basis, executives can't possibly have enough facts about a performer to know what to reinforce and what to ignore.

Rich Malloy, now retired, but an exemplar in the use of performance management at Kodak, was talking to some students in one of our performance management classes about MBWA and how important it is for supervisors to do. He confused them when he said that as a department manager he would never reinforce an operator's behavior. He explained that he had been away from frontline supervision so long that if he were to go on the floor and reinforce an operator for doing something exactly like he had wanted it done when he was a supervisor, he could easily get himself into hot water. Because of changes in procedures of which he may not be aware, he might inadvertently reinforce some behavior that the current supervisor was trying to change. I've asked many supervisors, "Has somebody from the front office ever come out and 'bragged on' an employee and created a problem for you?" Practically everyone answers with an emphatic, "Yes!"

A colleague, Tom Connellan (1978), tells about an automobile plant where the supervisor gave the performers an unscheduled break after they more than doubled their productivity. An executive, who just happened to be in the plant, saw the group on what he called an "unauthorized" break and chewed them out. Performance almost immediately fell to previous levels.

If you're an upper-level manager and you want to do MBWA in the plant or in the office, *at least* wander around with someone who knows what's happening there. Then *ask the supervisor or manager to point out behaviors and/or employees who deserve reinforcement.*

When you're on the floor, pay attention to the best performers *first.* Only after you've spent time with employees who are doing good things should you visit the area that was the initial target of your visit. Stop to recognize the good things first, even if you are on your way to see a specific problem. Then do the same thing on the way back through the plant. It takes very little time but pays dividends in terms of morale and productivity.

The best place to do MBWA is where you *know* that the performers are doing what they're supposed to do, usually the people who report directly to you. The further you get away from your direct reports, the more likely you are to create problems with aimless wondering/wandering. Do your homework first.

One more word on MBWA: an executive's first responsibility regarding reinforcement is to provide it for the people who directly report to him or her.

Mr. Toy Reid, now retired executive vice president of Eastman Chemical Company, asked me, "How much time should I spend attending team celebrations?"

I responded, "I don't know how you find the time to attend as many as you do." Even though he had an organization of over 10,000 employees, Reed rarely missed an opportunity to visit a team celebration.

I further suggested that he spend most of the time he had available for reinforcement with his management team and their direct reports. Not that he should never attend a frontline team celebration, but his primary MBWA should be at a different level.

Remember, reinforcement multiplies as it goes through the chain of command. Those who are reinforced tend to reinforce more often. If people at the top are getting reinforced, they are much more likely to reinforce those who work for them and so on through the organization. Don't bypass your direct reports!

Tough Times Demand Positive Reinforcement

The vice president of research and development at a southwestern telecommunications company was in trouble. His department had just missed several important product release dates. This crisis had been caused by faulty product releases prior to his appointment. No matter. This company had recently been acquired by a larger company with similar capabilities, and the president threatened to eliminate the department and turn its work over to the new parent company if it missed another release date.

Fortunately, this executive understood that negative reinforcement resulted in only incremental improvements, and incremental improvement would not save the department. He assembled all his managers and supervisors, who were being trained in performance management, and said, "We've lost the luxury of managing by negative reinforcement and punishment. As of Monday morning, I want a plan from each of you detailing how you will use positive reinforcement to get us out of this predicament."

Prior to this time, managers in this department had no mandate to use positive reinforcement. Although they were being trained in performance management techniques, and many were beginning to use them, some were not. With this new directive, all the managers began to put performance management to work.

Not only did the department not miss any more release dates, but the quality of the releases reached an all-time high. The department went on to become three times more efficient than the research department in the larger company.

While it's true that the vice president's directive had an implied threat, he used it as an antecedent to get behavior that could be positively reinforced. As his subordinate managers began to implement their plans, he provided them with frequent reinforcement, recognition, and celebrations.

Usually, tough times cause managers to get tough, meaning they crumble under pressure and use more punishment and negative reinforcement. It's a rare manager who has the understanding of behavioral concepts and the courage and foresight to use positive methods in the midst of a crisis. Remember that because positive reinforcement increases responding, when you are in a jam, you need a fast recovery, and only positive reinforcement can reliably deliver that. For the sake of American business, I hope that leaders like this vice president become more and more the rule and less the exception.

For an example of how long an initiative such as performance management lasts, see Gail Snyder, "Into the Millennium," *Performance Management Magazine* 16(1) (Winter 1998) and "Alabama 'Blues' Don't Sing the Blues Anymore," *Performance Management Magazine* 1(2). Blue Cross and Blue Shield of Alabama started implementing performance management in 1981 and continues to this day. It has continued to use performance management as a foundation for the way it designs and manages systems, processes, and management behaviors for over 35 years.

Epilogue

Performance Management and the Question of Values

Science is said to be amoral. Science can be used to invent instruments of healing or weapons of destruction. Lasers can be used in healing and in killing. Likewise, the laws of behavior can be used to make someone an ISIS terrorist, or a humanitarian, a confident leader or a hostile recluse. Reinforcement can be used to get people to do immoral, unethical, and illegal things. What, then, does this say about its propagation?

Immoral, unethical, and illegal behaviors have been occurring since the beginning of time. It is only now that we have the knowledge to arrange our environment to be able to affect these behaviors in a constructive and meaningful way. Could someone use this knowledge for harm or to increase ill-gotten gain? Yes. Is its potential harm reason to restrict its systematic use? To paraphrase B. F. Skinner, the best defense against tyranny is the education of everybody in the (behavioral) technology so that the power of reinforcement will not be in the hands of a few.

The performance management approach is value laden. Values come from behavior. They are statements about desirable behavior patterns that a group seeks to promote. To the extent that values can be pinpointed, they are much more achievable in any group, whether at home, at work, or in society in general. Let's examine some basic values and see how they relate to the concepts in this book.

Honesty

Honesty means that everything is aboveboard. There are no hidden agendas. The stated purpose of asking for a certain behavior or performance should be clear to everyone.

In performance management, there are no secrets. There is nothing in this book that you would not want everybody in your organization to know and use with each other and with you. The techniques in this book are not some secret method of getting people to work harder and not know it. Attempts at deception are shortsighted and do not bring out the best in people.

Some people think that if the performers know that you are using reinforcement, the reinforcement will not work. This is wrong. If what you are doing is reinforcing, it will work whether people know what you are doing or not.

If someone thanks me for doing a good job or laughs at my jokes, he or she may not be doing it to deliberately influence my future behavior. But to the extent that laughing at my jokes is reinforcing to me, I will respond like everybody else. I will do a good job again or tell more jokes.

Integrity and Trust

Performance management teaches that a manager should carefully follow up to make sure that the consequences match the antecedents. This is the basis for trust. The follow-up is to make sure that what the company *says* will happen after a certain behavior or performance *does* happen. This might be a positive consequence following good performance, or it might be a negative consequence following a poor performance. Either way, the credibility and integrity of the company are on the line. Trust is measured by the extent that management does what it says it is going to do.

Obviously, if a company has announced that bonuses will be paid for a certain goal attainment and then *doesn't* do it, it is teaching its employees not to trust it. Such a company need not be surprised when people are slow to give discretionary effort in the future.

Employees will be thinking, "Why put extra effort into the job? They don't mean what they say anyway! Remember when they promised us those bonuses? They didn't do what they promised. Why should we think this time is any different?" For that company's employees, the company will have demonstrated that it has no integrity and can't be trusted.

While trust is about predictability, integrity is more about living one's values. The integrity issue most often surfaces in less obvious ways. Often a company will announce, "We are committed to quality. Please tell us when there is a quality problem in your job because we want to make it right." Then, when someone points out a quality problem that necessitates stopping a production line or reworking a deficient product, that employee is told, "Oh, let that go. It will be okay. We are behind in our production today." This type of integrity problem can devastate a company and create a workforce for which integrity holds no meaning.

As you can see, integrity and trust are intertwined, and today, with the exponential increase in the ability of employees to know (and document) what is promised and what organizational values the company is committed to operate by, it is impossible to bring out the best without both.

Equality and Respect

The performance management approach implies a certain equality and respect in the way we approach another human being. The basic assumption in the approach is that most behavior is learned from consequences in the environment. Therefore, we conclude that there are logical reasons for the behavior of others: they act the way they do because they have *learned* to act that way.

Looking at behavior from this perspective, we are less likely to be judgmental in our estimation of others. Furthermore, we can begin to see that in many cases, we are part of the environment that *taught* our employees how to act that way! So, if we want to change the way *they* act, we must change their environment. While we may not be able to change much or the person's total environment, we can change the way we act when with the person.

Recognizing the universality of the laws of behavior also helps us to realize that *we* are as much a product of our environment as *they* are. We can understand the true meaning of the old saying, "There but for the grace of God go I."

We realize that if we had been punished for telling the truth, we might have become compulsive liars. If our work experience had come in a company where cheating the customer was common, we might be distrustful of others. If the consequences and events we had experienced in our family life had been different, we would also be different. This knowledge tends to make us a little more humble and a little more willing to take people as they are, without judging and condemning them.

This is not to say that we are *satisfied* to accept people as they are, only that we accept them as they are as a starting point, without trying to make them feel guilty about it. We learn to say, "Okay, this is where you are. Let's see what we can do to help you get better."

Whether we are addressing a poor performer or a good performer we say, "Let's see how we can help you get better." The only presumption we make is that anyone, no matter where he or she is now, *can be* better, including you and me.

Beyond the realization of equality is respect for what the other person brings to the party. Everybody has a unique perspective on life. It is unlike any other. It remains for us to capture it and enhance its value.

Justice

In a larger sense, the value of *justice* is also implied and promoted by performance management. Justice means that each person gets what he or she deserves. This is certainly what justice means in the courtroom sense. In performance management, this is what we say about managing people: *those who perform well and add value to the organization should get more reinforcement and rewards than those who perform poorly.*

In case after case in business and industry, low performers receive exactly the same compensation and recognition as high performers. The question higher performers ask, then, is a question of justice. "If we high performers are treated exactly the same as low performers, where is the fairness (justice) in that?" And, of course, after a while, they will stop performing at high levels (extinction). Thus the employer also ultimately gets what he or she deserves—low performance. Justice is served.

Further, giving poor performers the same reinforcement and rewards as better performers is not fair to the poor performers. Undeserved reinforcement and rewards maintain the poor performance. When management provides equal consequences for unequal performance, it actually robs the poor performers of the opportunity to improve.

Self-Esteem and Personal Growth

Reinforcement and rewards that are earned lead to higher self-esteem and personal growth. Earned recognition and rewards increase performers' feelings of confidence and competence. These performers have visible evidence that they add value to the organization. Confidence leads to an increase in initiative and a willingness to try new ideas. What organization can't profit from that?

Peace of Mind (Personal Security)

By pinpointing for people exactly which behaviors are wanted and the nature of the consequences of those behaviors, you encourage calm, well-thought-out decisions, and stress is reduced. When the relationship between behaviors and consequences is not clear, when people do not know how to earn positive consequences or how to avoid negative consequences, mental confusion and stress are the result.

Extensive studies have shown how noncontingent, random use of rewards and punishment produces "psychoses." The inconsistent, inexplicable application of consequences "drives people crazy." They never know which behaviors will be reinforced and which will be punished.

A client of mine described her boss's style as "jungle fighter." "You don't know exactly what he wants," she said, "and you never know when he is going to drop from the trees and surprise you." This is not good management, and it produces physical and mental stress.

When we are secure in knowing that right is rewarded and wrong is punished and we know which behaviors define each, we feel secure, calm, and confident because we are *in control of our own consequences!* Rewards come because we earn them, not through chance. Rather than wiggling helplessly in the clutch of fate, we can do something to help ourselves.

You can reduce the stress in your work environment simply by increasing positive reinforcement. You can increase security simply by letting people know through word and deed what will be reinforced and punished. The organizational benefits of a low-stress, secure workplace are well documented.

The Golden Rule

When positive reinforcement becomes a way of life in an organization, with reinforcement going from boss to subordinate, peer to peer, and peer to boss, adversarial relationships begin to disappear. People begin to treat each other as they would like to be treated.

When management believes that the way to get results is to threaten and punish, the counter-response from employees is to threaten and punish in return—often via unionization, sabotage, or reduced effort. Thus the classic *theory X* adversarial relationship is created. In contrast, when management demonstrates that the way to get the best results is to reinforce and reward improvement and to use punishment only to help poor performers improve, the counter-response from employees is to perform better and to seek more ways to get more reinforcement. In this way, a mutually reliant partnership is formed.

In this atmosphere, people learn that they can earn bigger rewards by working together than by resisting each other. This is what the various conflict-resolution and negotiation books call a win-win situation. When people are not operating out of the suspicion and fear generated by punishment and negative reinforcement, then they are better able to realize the benefits of working together. Remember what Sherman Roberts said: "The best way to run an organization is also the best way to treat people."

Performance Management in a Nutshell

Performance management focuses on the here and now. It is not an abstract, convoluted management principle with limited applications. *It is a precise, scientific approach that works!* There are no tricks or gimmicks. Unlike motivational theories, you don't need to delve into your workers' deep-seated feelings, anxieties, or motives. Performance management requires no psychoanalysis or role-playing. You don't need to find out what kind of childhood your performers had, what their birth orders were, or how they were raised. This approach accepts people as they are and deals with the behaviors in the present as a starting point. Because everyone operates under the same laws of behavior, applying these universal laws in a positive, effective way will bring about the behavior changes you are seeking in employees—whether you manage two people or 20,000.

References

Abernathy, W. B., *The Sin of Wages: Where the Conventional Pay System Has Led Us and How to Find a Way Out* (Memphis, TN: Abernathy & Associates, 1996).

Ainslie, G., "Specious Reward: A Behavioral Theory of Impulsiveness and Impulse Control," *Psychological Bulletin* 82 (1975): 463–496.

Alessi, G., "Diagnosis Diagnosed: A Systemic Reaction," *Professional School Psychology* 3(2) (1988): 145–151.

American Journalism Review, March 1993

American Quality Foundation, *International Quality Study* (IQS), San Antonio, TX, 1992.

Bailey, J., "The Rise, Decline and Fall of Educational Panaceas," unpublished research, University of Texas, Austin, TX, 1971, quoted by Ronald Zemke, "Bluffer's Guide to TQM," *Training*, April 1993, p. 48.

Berquam, E., "STRAT Analysis: Using Stratified Celeration Stacks to Summarize Charted Data," *Journal of Precision Teaching* 2(1) (April 1981): 13–17.

Binder, C., "Fluency Building," PT/MS, Inc., Nonantum, MA, 1987.

Coles, G., "The Learning Disabilities Test Battery: Empirical and Social Issues," *Harvard Educational Review* 48 (1978): 313–340.

Connellan, T. K., *How to Improve Human Performance: Behaviorism in Business and Industry* (New York: Harper & Row, 1978).

Cordery, J. I., Mueller, W. S., and Smith, L. M., "Attitudinal and Behavioral Effects of Autonomous Group Working: A Longitudinal Study," *Academy of Management Journal* 34(2) (1991): 464–475.

Crosby, P., *Quality Is Free: The Art of Making Quality Certain* (New York: New American Library, 1979).

Daniels, A. C., and Bailey, J. S., *Performance Management: Changing Behavior the Drives Organizational Effectiveness* (Atlanta: Performance Management Publications, 2012).

Davison, M., and McCarthy, D., "The Matching Law," research review, cited by *REAPS DataSharing Newsletter*, Behavior Prosthesis Laboratory, Waltham, MA, March 1981.

Deming, W. E., *Out of the Crisis* (Cambridge, MA: MIT Press, 1986).

Employee Involvement Association (EIA), 1990 study, Dayton, OH, 1990.

Engelmann, S., *War Against the Schools' Academic Child Abuse* (Portland, OR: Halcyon House, 1992).

Engelmann, S., and Carnine, D. W., *Theory of Instruction* (New York: Irvington, 1982).

Ericsson, K. A., and Charness, N., "Expert Performance: Its Structure and Acquisition," *American Psychologist* (August 1994): 725–747.

Ernst & Young Study, cited by *The Wall Street Journal*.

Gilbert, T., *Human Competence: Engineering Worthy Performance* (New York: McGraw-Hill, 1978).

Green, L., Myerson, J., and Ostaszewski, P., "Amount of Reward Has Opposite Effects on the Discounting of Delayed and Probabilistic Outcomes," *Journal of Experimental Psychology* 25(2) (March 1999), 418–427.

Hart, B., and Risley, T. R., *Meaningful Differences in the Everyday Experience of Young American Children* (Baltimore, MD: Paul H. Brookes, 1995).

Haughton, E., *REAPS DataSharing Newsletter*, Behavior Prosthesis Laboratory, Waltham, MA, March 1981.

Henkoff, R., "Cost-Cutting: How to Do It Right," *Fortune*, April 9, 1991, pp. 40–49.

Herrnstein, R. J., "Rational Choice Theory," *American Psychologist* 45(3) (March 1990): 356–367.

Herrnstein, R., "The Relative and Absolute Strength of Response as a Function of Frequency of Reinforcement," *Journal of Experimental Analysis of Behavior* 4 (1961): 267–272.

Herzburg, F., Mauser, B., and Snyderman, B., *The Motivation to Work* (New York: Wiley, 1959).

Honeywell, J. A., Dickinson, A. M., and Poling, A., "Individual Performance as a Function of Individual and Group Pay Contingencies," *Psychological Record* 47 (1997): 261–274.

Hopkins, B., et al., "A Digest of Some of the Literature on Self-Managed Work Groups," unpublished study, Auburn University, Auburn, AL, 1992.

Ivarie, J., "Effects of Proficiency Rates on Later Performance of a Recall and Writing Behavior," *RASE* 7(5) (September–October 1986): 25–30.

Johnson, K. R., and Layng, T. V. J., "Breaking the Structuralist Barrier: Literacy and Numeracy with Fluency," *American Psychologist* 47(11) (November 1992): 1475–1490.

Kohn, A., *Punished by Rewards* (Boston: Houghton Mifflin, 1993).

Komaki, J., "Toward Effective Supervision: An Operant Analysis and Comparison of Managers at Work," *Journal of Applied Psychology* 71(2) (1986): 270–279.

Land, G., *Grow or Die: The Unifying Principles of Transformation* (New York: Dell, 1973).

Latham, G., "The Application of Behaviorological Principles in School Settings at Home and Abroad: The Worst of the Best at Best," *Behaviorological Commentaries* (Summer 1992): 3–10.

Levering, R., and Moskowitz, M., *The 100 Best Companies to Work for in America* (New York: Currency/Doubleday, 1993).

Lindsley, O., "B. F. Skinner—Mnemonic for His Contributions to Precision Teaching," *Journal of Precision Teaching* 3 (1991): 2–7.

Lindsley, O., "Dangers of Percent and How to Avoid Them," unpublished paper, Behavior Research Co., Lawrence, KS, 1994.

Lindsley O., "What We Know That Ain't So," invited address, Third Convention, Midwestern Association for Behavior Analysis, Chicago, IL, 1977.

London, M., and Oldham, G. R., "A Comparison of Group and Individual Incentive Plans," *Academy of Management Journal* 20 (1977): 34–41.

Maddox, J., *What Remains to Be Discovered: Mapping the Secrets of the Universe, the Origins of Life, and the Future of the Human Race* (New York: Free Press, 1998).

Madsen, C. H., Jr., and Madsen, C. R., *Teaching and Discipline: Behavior Principles Toward a Positive Approach* (Boston: Allyn & Bacon, 1974).

Mayer, R. R., and Pipe, P., *Analyzing Performance Problems or "You Really-Oughta-Wanna"* (Belmont, CA: Fearon-Pittman Publishers, 1970).

Miller, A. D., and Heward, W. L., "Do Your Students Really Know Their Math Facts?" *Intervention in School and Clinic* 28 November 1992: 98–104.

Peters, C., "Intern Leadership Conference," Disney World, Ernst & Young, Tampa, FL, August 1999.

Peters, T., *Thriving on Chaos: Handbook for a Management Revolution* (New York: HarperCollins, 1988).

Peters, T. J., and Waterman, R. H., *In Search of Excellence* (New York: Harper & Row, 2004).

Premack, D., "Toward Empirical Behavior Laws: I. Positive Reinforcement," *Psychological Review* 66 (1959): 219–233.

Schmidt, R. A., *Motor Learning and Performance: From Principles to Practice* (Windsor, Ontario, Canada: Human Kinetics, 1991).

Schneider, W., "Training High-Performance Skills: Fallacies and Guidelines," *Human Factors* 27(3) (1985): 285–300.

Senge, P., *The Fifth Discipline: The Art and Practice of the Learning Organization* (New York: Doubleday/Currency, 1990).

Skinner, B. F., *The Technology of Teaching* (Englewood Cliffs, NJ: Prentice-Hall, 1969).

Skinner, B. F., *Walden Two* (Indianapolis: Hackett Publishing, 1976).

Snyder, G., "Morningside Academy: A Learning Guarantee," *Performance Management Magazine* 10 (1992): 29–35.

Stuart, R. B., "Assessment and Change of the Communication Patterns of Juvenile Delinquents and Their Parents," in *Advances of Behavior Therapy* (New York: Academic Press, 1971).

Tapscott, D., *Growing Up Digital: The Rise of the Net Generation* (New York: McGraw-Hill, 1999).

Thomas, D. R., Becker, W. C., and Armstrong, M., "Production and Elimination of Disruptive Classroom Behavior by Systematically Varying Teacher's Behavior," *Journal of Applied Behavior Analysis* 1(1) (1968): 35–45.

Training Magazine Annual Report, October 1992.

Watkins, C. L., *Project Follow-Through: A Case Study of Contingencies Influencing Instructional Practices of the Educational Establishment* (Cambridge, MA: Cambridge Center for Behavioral Studies, 1997).

White, M. A., "Natural Rates of Teacher Approval and Disapproval in the Classroom," *Journal of Applied Behavior Analysis* 8(4) (1975): 367–372.

"Wilson Learning Corporation Study," *Training and Development Journal*, February 1993.

Wingert, P., "The Sum of Mediocrity," *Newsweek*, December 6, 1996, p. 96.

Index

About the Author

Aubrey Daniels, a thought leader and internationally recognized expert on management, leadership, safety, and workplace issues, is considered an authority on human behavior in the workplace. As founder and chairman of the board of his consulting firm, Aubrey Daniels International, he and his staff help organizations employ the timeless principles of behavioral science to reenergize the workplace, optimize performance, and achieve lasting results. Aubrey actively blogs about performance systems, workplace safety, and management issues; is frequently interviewed for major media outlets; and pens a regular guest blog for *Talent Management Magazine*.

In addition to being a highly sought-after keynote speaker at major association, conference, and educational events, Aubrey is the author of six bestselling books widely recognized as international management classics: *Bringing Out the Best in People: How to Apply the Astonishing Power of Positive Reinforcement, Performance Management: Changing Behavior That Drives Organizational Effectiveness, Other People's Habits: How to Use Positive Reinforcement to Bring Out the Best in People Around You, Measure of a Leader, OOPs! 13 Management Practices That Waste Time & Money (and what to do instead),* and *Safe by Accident: Take the Luck Out of Safety—Leadership Practices that Build a Sustainable Safety Culture.* His books have been translated into Japanese, Chinese, Korean, Spanish, and French and have been licensed in China, India, Indonesia, Italy, Japan, Korea, Romania, and Saudi Arabia. He is also founder and editor of the *Journal of Organizational Behavior Management* (1980); founder and publisher of *Performance Management Magazine* (1982), now *PM eZine*; and recipient of numerous awards and honors, including Fellow, International Association for Behavior Analysis. He is chairman of the Aubrey Daniels Institute, which is dedicated to increasing the understanding and advancing the use of the science of behavior (behavior analysis) in the workplace. Dr. Daniels has been an associate professor and lecturer at the Kennedy

School of Government of Harvard University and a visiting professor at Florida State University. He was a founding board member of the Cambridge Center for Behavioral Studies and is active in the Association for Behavior Analysis International (ABAI). He has also served on the Alumni Board of Furman University, his alma mater.

About Aubrey Daniels International

Founded in 1978 and headquartered in Atlanta, GA, Aubrey Daniels International (ADI) provides clients with the tools and methodologies to help move people toward positive, results-driven accomplishments and improve their business:

- **Assessments:** scientific analyses of the impact of systems, processes, structures, and practices
- **Expert consulting:** specialized, hands-on direction and support
- **Executive coaching:** helping executives apply a behavioral lens to improve their impact on others and the organization
- **Coaching for Rapid Change®:** a systematic process for focusing managers and leaders to shape positive actions
- **Surveys:** a complete suite of proprietary surveys
- **Safety solutions:** surveys, assessments, behavior-based safety, and safety leadership training and coaching
- **Seminars and webinars:** a variety of engaging programs
- **Scorecards and incentive pay:** an alternative to traditional incentive pay systems
- **Certification:** ADI-endorsed mastery of client skills in our key products, processes, and/or technology
- **Speakers:** accredited and celebrated thought leaders
- **Blitz Precision Learning®:** web-based application for developing, delivering, and administering training lessons

For further information, please visit www.aubreydaniels.com.